OUR BLOC

JAMES SCHNEIDER co-founded Momentum in 2015 and went on to serve as Jeremy Corbyn's spokesperson and head of strategic communications. He is communications director for the Progressive International and a regular voice in the UK media.

OUR BLOC: HOW WE WIN

James Schneider

VERSO

London • New York

First published by Verso 2022
© James Schneider 2022
An earlier version of Chapter 1 appeared as 'Bridging the
Gap: Corbynism after Corbyn', in Grace Blakeley, ed.,
Futures of Socialism, London and New York, 2020.

1 3 5 7 9 10 8 6 4 2

Verso
UK: 6 Meard Street, London W1F 0EG
US: 388 Atlantic Avenue, Brooklyn, NY 11217
versobooks.com

Verso is the imprint of New Left Books

ISBN-13: 978-1-83976-850-7
ISBN-13: 978-1-83976-879-8 (US EBK)
ISBN-13: 978-1-83976-878-1 (UK EBK)

British Library Cataloguing in Publication Data
A catalogue record for this book is available from the British Library

Library of Congress Cataloging-in-Publication Data

Names: Schneider, James J. (James Joseph), 1947– author.
Title: Our bloc : how we win / James Schneider.
Description: London ; New York : Verso Books, 2022. | Includes
  bibliographical references.
Identifiers: LCCN 2022021317 (print) | LCCN 2022021318 (ebook) | ISBN
  9781839768507 (paperback) | ISBN 9781839768798 (ebk)
Subjects: LCSH: Right and left (Political science) – Great Britain. |
  Coalitions – Great Britain. | Socialism – Great Britain. | Labour Party
  (Great Britain) | Labor unions – Political activity – Great Britain. |
  Social movements – Political aspects – Great Britain. | Great
  Britain – Politics and government – 21st century.
Classification: LCC JN1122 .S35 2022 (print) | LCC JN1122 (ebook) | DDC
  320.50941 – dc23/eng/20220603
LC record available at https://lccn.loc.gov/2022021317
LC ebook record available at https://lccn.loc.gov/2022021318

Typeset in Garamond by Biblichor Ltd, Scotland
Printed and bound by CPI Group (UK) Ltd, Croydon, CR0 4YY

This book is dedicated to David Graeber and Leo Panitch, two great friends and guides we lost in 2020.

Contents

Introduction

Defeatism plagues the British left, disorienting those who came together to support the programme and politics advanced by Labour under Jeremy Corbyn. Some maintain that we should stay and fight against Labour's resurgent neo-Blairites, but offer few clues for how to prevail against them.[1] Others argue that socialists need a new electoral vehicle that will at least give activists something to do in a party whose leadership doesn't despise them.[2] There are also those who say we should abandon the electoral path altogether and throw ourselves into resistance to capitalism's various predations through semi-spontaneous movements which may come and go. The financial crisis may have created an opening for left-populist electoral advance, but this crack has been plastered over by Boris Johnson's 'Get Brexit Done' revolution from above. The closed national aperture is mirrored inside Labour, whose leadership seeks to place the party's left in a 'sealed tomb'.[3]

If these three paths sound familiar, it is because they are retreats to the strategies of the pre-Corbyn era, acts of self-marginalisation after a period when socialist ideas and organising jostled for national centre stage. In short, they say, 'We tried, we failed, let's go back to how we did things before.' Though the landscape may appear ugly, it should not precipitate descent into left melancholia.[4] Despair is a betrayal – not only because hope is a responsibility for those on the left, but also because the objective situation is not wretched. In 2015, out of an apparently sad scene – thirty-five years of trade union decline, an anti-war movement that was unable to stop wars, an anti-austerity movement that couldn't prevent cuts, a Labour left so marginal as to barely be noticed, a panoply of groupuscules with little connection to mainstream society, a Green Party with a solitary MP, and a national political debate dominated by budget deficits and migration targets – rose a challenge to the system that raised the hopes of millions and frightened the rich and powerful.

We found our opportunity to advance by accident. Corbyn was elected Labour leader as an extreme outsider, at a moment of historic weakness for the organised left, through a selection process that its designers had hoped would extinguish dissent but instead aided it. Progressive forces had limited raw material with which to mount a significant advance on state power, and yet Corbyn really did nearly become prime minister. Almost 13 million people voted for the social-democratic change described in the 2017 manifesto. Following that vote, Labour polled around 40 per cent for eighteen months.[5] The Corbyn project sought to build a social majority around a common agenda. Ultimately, it was able neither to stimulate sufficient social forces to organise this majority, nor to overcome the contradictions of Brexit. But we must never lose sight of that goal: constructing a social majority for change with a political vehicle and the organised forces in society – trade unions, social movements, progressive organisations and campaigns – to carry it out.

In the 2010s, for the first time in many years, socialists in the major capitalist states had a serious shot at winning office. Leo Panitch summarised it as a turn 'from protest to politics'.[6] A radical electoral surge across the Global North not only saw Jeremy Corbyn approach Downing Street but also Bernie Sanders threaten the White House and Jean-Luc Mélenchon dream of the Élysée Palace, while Pablo Iglesias could promise a *sorpasso* and Alexis Tsipras take office in Athens pledging to resist the financial waterboarding of the troika. That surge has run its course for now. But it has left behind a stronger set of progressive forces, with greater potential for advance. Within the British Labour Party, the right is in the ascendancy, but not because socialist ideas have been rejected. Rather, Keir Starmer won the leadership on a false prospectus and has driven the party away from the labour and social movements that could sustain it.

While the tip of our transformative spear has been blunted with Labour's return to the mean, the ruling class is not fundamentally secure. Public attitudes show little support for the status quo, obliging Boris Johnson to present himself as an agent of change.[7] The conditions that gave rise to Corbyn's leadership, and the braver and more challenging political formation he represented, have not gone away. Inequality grows while living standards fall, and the climate emergency has reached its 'now or never' moment after the failure of COP26 in Glasgow.[8] The ruling class can't work out how to overcome neoliberalism's mounting contradictions. Climate shocks, rising debt, inequality and energy costs are hard barriers to the existing system's viability. 'You will own nothing and be happy' is the tin-eared offering to the masses from the World Economic Forum.[9]

Changing the world without taking power is a luxury unavailable to us. The pandemic has made plain that the state is essential in upholding the socio-economic order. In 2020 the coordinated action by the big four central banks – the US Federal Reserve, European Central Bank, Bank of Japan and Bank of England – to create $9 trillion through quantitative easing, the largest economic state intervention in human history, increased the wealth of the world's billionaires by over 50 per cent.[10] The policy was carried out with practically zero democratic oversight or popular input. Surging billionaire wealth is evidence that state policy is central to capitalist accumulation, alongside extraction of value from workers and environmental and social exploitation. The billionaire class has neither the plans, the technology, nor the will to avert climate catastrophe or looming energy and resource shortages, a foretaste of which we are experiencing today.[11] The need for rapid and fundamental change is clear. And there can be no rapid and fundamental change without seizing the state's levers.[12] That we failed last time must not cloud our focus on the state: if we aren't preparing to use power, someone else will.

Despite our various defeats, now is not the moment to scale back our ambitions. Rather, we can rethink them for these new times. The situation demands action – not just to meet people's immediate needs, but also because the weakness of the ruling class's grip on events presents an opportunity for system change. No one will meet this moment for us. To break from our shackles, we need to develop a strategy to win. The relative capacities and organisation of competing social forces will inform who takes advantage of contingent political openings. 'Be ready! Be ready for the improbable, for the unexpected, for what happens,' said the French Marxist Daniel Bensaïd.[13] We cannot know what those contingent openings will be, but the strength that popular and elite forces can bring to bear will be decisive in the outcome.

For the British left to win, I argue for a strategy that places a premium on organising progressive social forces – the movements and potential movements that wrestle with power – under a common banner, so that they are stronger in their individual struggles and able to mobilise a wider mass of the population in favour of key demands. No political party is undertaking this work, and yet it must be done. Yes, at some stage we will need an electoral vehicle that can win and take office to enact wide-reaching reforms. But first we need an entity that can begin to unite and mobilise towards a social majority. The Italian revolutionary theorist Antonio Gramsci called this social majority, once formed, a 'historic bloc'. It won't just be thrown together automatically by economic or social developments, because the dead weight of ideological inertia tends to hold things back. Instead, active political construction is needed – the ironing out of internal tensions between constituent groups by identification of shared interests.[14]

I argue that the post-Corbyn British left must actively construct a left bloc: a formal, explicit alliance of social movements, trade unions, the Labour grassroots and socialists in Parliament to make our voices louder and our organising more effective. To develop this strategy, we must first see where we have come from. So Chapter 1 looks back at Corbynism to examine the gap between that moment's possibilities and our movement's strength. From this point, we look forward. Chapter 2 assesses the strengths and weaknesses of our opponents through an analysis of the Conservative Party under Johnson and Labour's rightward turn under Starmer. Chapter 3 shows how a left bloc might be assembled, and Chapter 4 lays out in practical terms what it could achieve by following what I call a movement populist approach – an adaptation of the theory of left populism developed by Chantal Mouffe and Ernesto Laclau. Chapter 5 looks ahead to the sort of new model party that might articulate the needs of our combined progressive movements, and sets out a strategy for democratising the state.

We can't know what the future holds, and we may not feel optimistic. We suffer from an authoritarian government, a supine opposition, a decade of seemingly futile resistance, and more hardship to come as prices and bills shoot ahead of wages. But for the underdog, winning always seems impossible until it happens. History doesn't move in straight lines – it zigs and zags. Each progressive surge builds the capacities for the next in ways that are often hard to fathom at the time. The defeat of the Corbyn movement hurt, but the experience has given us resources we couldn't have dreamed of before. We cannot call into existence progressive forces that aren't there. We can't click our fingers and manifest the perfect vehicle for socialist advance. Instead, we must strengthen what we have, support what's emerging and bring it all together more effectively.

Social contest toggles between two phases: surges and struggles for influence. The Corbyn period mainly followed one phase, the surge. Surges involve direct and dramatic confrontation between social forces, where the balance of power can shift rapidly as one side wins out. These are intense, urgent moments when the impact of actions can be felt almost immediately. The second phase is the fight for influence, which constructs the terrain on which future surges will be fought. Rather than sitting around waiting for the next surge, we seek to advance the progressive position and tighten our organisation in every way we can. This work is vital, if less instantly gratifying.[15]

Another progressive surge is inevitable: the contradictions in the global system are too numerous to suggest otherwise. Constructing a left bloc following the 'movement populist' strategy puts us in the best position to seize the opportunities and shield ourselves from the threats that arise. We have it in our power to end the 2020s with progressive forces better prepared to wrest control from the few. Success could take many forms. The final chapter of this book sketches four versions of winning written from the vantage point of the close of the decade. In some, the Labour Party is central; in others, it is an irrelevance. Each one envisages progressive forces coming together in novel and dynamic formations.

To keep the possibilities open and turn winning from a distant hope into a reality, we must use the coming years to build power, weaken our opponents, and prepare ourselves for the next surge.

The First Surge

What was Corbynism, that distinct and vertiginous period of socialist advance and eventual electoral defeat? And more importantly, what is in store for the movement that rode a great, exhilarating wave of possibility?

Every participant in Jeremy Corbyn's 2015 leadership campaign will admit that the surge in support took them by surprise.[1] In May 2015, after Labour's election defeat and the resignation of party leader Ed Miliband, the leader of the Labour left, John McDonnell, proclaimed that moment 'the darkest hour that socialists in Britain had faced since the Attlee government fell in 1951'.[2] Three weeks later, Jeremy Corbyn was on stage with three New Labour continuity candidates at *Newsnight*'s televised hustings, visibly winning over an audience of former Labour voters in Tory-held Nuneaton with his unpolished message of peace, public ownership and democracy.

The mechanics of how Corbyn catapulted from 200 to 1 outsider to leader of a mostly hollowed out Labour Party have been well covered.[3] Suffice it to say that the campaign wasn't won because the Labour left was well organised or used to winning. Rather, Corbyn's candidature became an expression of the interests, talents and energy of the UK's progressive forces – the labour, peace, anti-racist, feminist, anti-austerity, climate and tenants' movements. A wave from below powered the campaign, and Corbyn rode it to the finish line. That the left got so far, however, indicated not just our budding strength, but also the relatively sudden fragility of our opponents: the ruling class and its witting and unwitting agents of control.

While the basic coordinates of the economic and political system were unchanged following the 2008 financial crisis, the status quo was at its most open to challenge in a generation. The 2015 British Social Attitudes survey found that over half of the British public thought the government did not much care 'what people like me think'. The 2016 survey showed that close to half the population supported higher levels of spending on health, education and social security. Dissatisfaction with the status quo, though inchoate, was rife.

But the political-media class looked at the majority won by David Cameron's Conservatives in the 2015 general election – 11.3 million votes, 37 per cent of the total – and saw an endorsement of the status quo. The columnists and focus group pedlars weren't looking at what was hiding in plain sight. The 4 million votes for UKIP, support for Scottish independence leading to SNP's near clean sweep in Scotland, the Green Party's rapid pre-election membership growth and the expansion and vitality of the anti-austerity and student movements – all this signalled an appetite for change, bouncing off in many directions. It needed only an effective vehicle to cohere and unlock it.

Corbyn victorious

'We don't have to be unequal. It doesn't have to be unfair,' Corbyn proclaimed in his acceptance speech following the 2015 Labour leadership election. 'Things can, and they will, change.' This powerful statement of possibility filled the lungs of socialists and progressives across the country. It also revealed a weakness: who would do the changing? The expression typified the central challenge for the Corbyn project. Yes, the system was struggling to reproduce itself; but no, we were not yet the cause. Between the circumstances of systemic fragility and the relative weakness of progressive social forces there opened a gap – which Corbynism occupied.

The task of the Corbyn project was to occupy that gap for as long as possible while building up progressive social forces. It was an enormous undertaking: forty years of defeat for the left had fundamentally reshaped society. The Labour Party was cartelised, local government hollowed out and Westminster insulated from pressure from below. Tenants had been stripped of protections and a voice. The peace, anti-racist, feminist and ecological movements advanced, but had yet to join forces. And the once powerful organised working class had been reduced to a residue, as the wage share of national income fell from almost two-thirds to just over half. The balance of forces was decidedly unfavourable.

Corbyn's leadership offered an opportunity to arrest this historic decline and lead a new advance. But to spur on a movement while desperately hanging on to office was a colossal challenge. Corbyn's allies were few: three fellow members of the shadow cabinet; less than a tenth of Labour MPs; an understaffed office; a new organisation, Momentum, with neither money, governance structures nor an agreed strategy; and a relatively weak organised trade union and social-movement left. The mass of the membership and the weight of Unite, at least, were on his side. The scale of hostility he faced from the media and Labour's anti-socialists, on the other hand, was extreme and unprecedented. John McDonnell liked to refer to the Gramsci-inspired concept of struggle 'in and against the state'. Before Corbyn got close to Downing Street, however, he would have to struggle in and against the party.

In the summer of 2016, the anti-socialists committed a great mistake: by orchestrating an attempted coup, they propelled the unorganised elements supporting Corbyn to join forces with Unite and Momentum. The 2016 leadership campaign didn't just strengthen Corbyn's mandate, securing the project's continued occupation of the gap; it also reduced the gap by further strengthening, educating and organising progressive forces around a common project for power.

A similar pattern repeated itself in the following year's general election. Corbyn's campaigning skill, the party's popular policies and the quirks of British electoral broadcasting rules, which focus attention on parties' top leaderships, drew a new, central dividing line: Corbyn's Labour against austerity Conservatives. That allowed Corbyn to be heard on issue after issue advocating popular social-democratic policies. Just two years before, such proposals – scrapping tuition fees, ending austerity, taking utilities into public ownership, increasing taxes on the rich – had been politically marginal. In 2017 they re-entered the mainstream. Labour's 13 million votes didn't secure victory, but the largest vote share increase since 1945 kept Corbyn in office and dramatically shifted political discourse. The campaign organised, educated and empowered the movement, which began properly to contemplate government for the first time. The gap between possibility and power closed substantially.[4]

In the next two and a half years, grassroots power was felt unevenly across the party and many MPs remained hostile, but the National Executive Committee now had a socialist majority and appointed a socialist, Jennie Formby, to head up the party bureaucracy. Several socialists were hired into the party's staff and Momentum's staff also grew on the back of its 40,000-strong membership, swelling experience and capacity on the left.

Change came slowly at best in most regional offices and in the party's elections department, which fiercely resisted the formation of a new community organising unit that was central to a long-term socialist strategy. By 2019 more Labour councils were trying to deliver municipal social democracy, but local government was still far from embodying socialist hope and resistance. Reforms to how MPs are selected by local parties were a flop, and the party's Democracy Review democratised little. Momentum, Unite and the Communication Workers Union (CWU) secured the selection of left candidates in about half of Labour's target seats; however, the party's 'preparing for government' exercise was, while detailed, fatally flawed. It tended to treat Corbyn's programme as something which could be implemented by the existing state machinery, without mass mobilisations, and failed to take into account the likely extent of establishment backlash.

If party reform tended to be top-down, political education would have to come from below: neither the party, nor Momentum, nor Unite put together a substantial programme. Proposals for turning Young Labour into a 'university of the working class' never got off the ground.[5] The World Transformed, on the other hand, was the most vibrant part of the conference every year and spawned several local festivals across the country. The novel prospect of state power turbocharged the Corbynite intellectual space: books with plans for power, such as Christine Berry and Joe Guinan's *People Get Ready* and Grace Blakeley's *Stolen: How to Save the World from Financialisation*, were published in 2019; *Tribune* and Novara expanded their output; and there was a boom in left-friendly think tanks.

In the economic realm, the Corbyn period saw a limited advance for progressive forces. After decades of decline, trade union membership stopped falling and began to rise – although overall membership still skews towards public sector, better-paid and older workers – and trade unions were substantially relegitimised in public discourse. Although organisations such as ACORN, Generation Rent and the London Renters Union made progress, a national tenants' movement remained a long way off. No new working-class social institutions have replaced the past's dense lattice of everyday solidarity.

Media hostility remained intense, often to the point of absurdity, but more socialist voices and perspectives were included in current affairs programming. Public discourse and political common sense as a whole shifted, though critical mass culture on television and radio remained much rarer than it was in the 1970s. Grime, a musical genre whose artists and fans broadly backed the change that Corbyn offered, was one bright spot, providing anti-establishment messages – 'Fuck the government and fuck Boris,' as Stormzy raps in chart-topping 'Vossi Bop' – for mass audiences.

The peace, anti-racist and feminist movements all remained energetic, even as a number of their activists were drawn into Labour-focused work. The ecological movement advanced dramatically during Corbyn's tenure, though not (despite his sincere and longstanding personal commitment to environmentalism) because of it. Indeed, Labour was quiet on environmental issues until 2019 when – under tremendous pressure from below, from youth climate strikers, Extinction Rebellion and Labour for a Green New Deal – it finally took a leadership role, forcing Parliament to declare a climate emergency and developing and championing ambitious policies.[6] This striking shift in direction and tempo revealed the possibilities for a party porous to movement demands.

All considered, the progressive movement inside and outside the party was substantially more developed on the eve of the 2019 general election than it had been in 2017 or 2015. This capacity was evident in the campaign, when both Momentum and the elements of the party machine that weren't hostile to the membership organised an impressive number of activists. At the moment of electoral mobilisation, the grassroots was strong. But by then the leadership had run out of steam, worn down and fractured by Brexit.

Corbyn defeated

In two and a half years of battles on the issue of Brexit, Corbyn never found ground he could hold. Usually on the retreat, he was left arguing for compromise for its own sake, with the Brexit policy defined by neither democratic socialist principle nor strategic electoral viability. Brexit gave the establishment a wedge to drive into the heart of the Corbyn project, and it did so with glee. Its repertoire – round-the-clock attacks, accusations of idiocy, performative confusion – need not be rehearsed. Within the party, those who both supported Corbyn and wished to overturn the referendum result acted as the establishment's dupes. They wanted Corbyn to make the anti-democratic, Europhile argument that he never convincingly could. By the 2019 general election, Corbyn had lost his room for manoeuvre and his team was fundamentally divided on how to play an extremely challenging hand. The burnish of 2017, when Corbyn had appeared a politician apart, authentically himself, had been painfully wiped off.

In 2017, by focusing on class antagonism and offering a set of popular policies, Corbyn's Labour dominated the left half of the political spectrum, sweeping aside the social reformers and liberals. In 2019, Labour won 10.3 million votes, more than in five of the last ten general elections, but fewer seats than in any since 1935. The discrepancy can be explained primarily by the semi-floating signifier of Brexit.[7] Boris Johnson's Conservatives brutally dominated the right half of politics by purging and sidelining any members of their party squeamish about the government's Brexit strategy, and cajoling the Brexit Party to stand down in every Tory-held seat. Europe was the defining issue, and the Conservatives' 'Get Brexit Done' slogan brought together diverse voter groups – those who hated the EU, those who hated politicians and those weary of the Brexit debate. Labour was left promising that substantial change could come through the ballot box – just not the substantial change a majority voted for in the 2016 referendum.

Corbyn's tenure is now long over, but the situation should not cause socialists to despair. Labour is not and never has been a socialist party. But over four and a half years, socialist leadership provided a project for power for progressive forces to work towards. The challenge for these forces is to keep growing – and to pull in roughly the same direction – now that there is little leadership and no single strategic horizon.

The Corbyn movement may feel orphaned but it is no infant. It can succeed if it proves its maturity through tolerance for diversity, internal generosity and commitment to the long haul. Corbyn's leadership was never going to bring socialism, even if elected with a majority government. It was a spark, a staging post, the beginning of an organised movement. It is up to all of us to take the cause further and win advances, for the many, not the few. We can prove Jeremy Corbyn right: there is no such thing as Corbynism; there is socialism.[8] And things can, and they will, change.

2

Capital's A and B Teams

Those surveying the political horizon and seeing eternal Tory rule should look back to 2018, at a party falling apart amid mounting contradictions. Under Theresa May, the September 2018 Conservative conference was full of fringe discussions asking if the Tories were doomed as renters and younger voters flocked to Labour. In one meeting, the Conservative MP George Freeman posed the central question facing capitalist hegemony: 'Why would you ever be a capitalist if you've got no chance of ever getting any capital?'[1]

This Tory panic was not just hysteria created by the hothouse environment of conference season. Its proximate cause was Corbyn's success in reshaping British politics, but Corbyn's success in turn had deeper roots.[2] The disastrous war in Iraq and the 2008 financial crisis frayed consent in the neoliberal order; that process was articulated politically in their different ways by Vote Leave and a socialist-led Labour Party. We had entered what Gramsci called an organic crisis, when cracks emerge and spread across the fresco of capitalist rule. In this chapter, I look at how Boris Johnson and Keir Starmer have attempted to prop up their respective ends of the Westminster consensus, and argue that the crisis of British politics-as-usual is not over yet.

Organic crises

The last systemic crisis in Britain played out inside the governing Labour party in the late 1970s, as the post-war consensus – the political economy and class compromise of the previous thirty years – broke down. Three tendencies emerged, each proposing a different path through the crisis. Foreign Secretary Anthony Crosland, author of the revisionist classic *The Future of Socialism* (1956), which made the case for social-democratic acclimatisation to affluent consumer capitalism, held that the best course of action was to hold one's nerve and carry on as before. On the left, by contrast, Tony Benn argued for capital controls and an expanded and democratised public sector: a radicalisation of social democracy, which among other things would have required the UK to free itself from the constraints of the Common Market. A third and dominant tendency, however, led by the chancellor Denis Healey and the prime minister James Callaghan, opted instead to abandon Keynesian deficit financing for proto-monetarist austerity. Callaghan sounded the death knell for post-war social democracy at Labour's 1976 conference, winning praise from the godfather of neoliberalism, Milton Friedman. Crises are warnings as well as opportunities: this one was resolved in a reactionary direction that anticipated the Thatcherite onslaught.

How does the present crisis compare? The Conservatives have been in government since 2010, increasing their vote at each of the last four general elections. But we live in a time of substantial voter volatility: four different political parties have led in the polls in that period and Scotland has politically become another country entirely, with the Scottish National Party dominant in the once-rock-solid Labour central belt. Westminster Tories of the post–New Labour era have not managed to create a durable historic bloc: a ruling-class settlement that engenders sufficient consent in other sections of society to guarantee social peace.

The first attempt to build one, under Cameron, combined the punitive logic of austerity with migrant-baiting and a dose of cosmopolitan social liberalism. This approach brought success in the 2015 election as the Tories gobbled up their coalition partner's seats and watched as Labour was wiped out in Scotland for campaigning alongside them in the previous year's independence referendum. But this electoral success was too thin to paper over the cracks for long. A revolt on the right – UKIP and the Leave campaign – increasingly challenged the Cameron leadership's commitment to cosmopolitan social liberalism, while the material effect of austerity on living standards (and a Labour Party at last willing to represent those affected) shattered the austerity discourse that had so dominated politics.

After the 2016 Brexit referendum, there were at least two alternative political tendencies to Continuity Cameronism within the Conservative Party. On the libertarian right, International Trade Secretary Liam Fox advocated extending the reach of neoliberalism through extreme post-Brexit deregulation. A right–populist strand, meanwhile, seems to have regarded the end of the neoliberal economic model as inevitable, but sought to lead the change. Presenting herself as the answer to the crisis of austerity, in her first speech as prime minister Theresa May listed seven 'burning injustices' it was her government's mission to fight. She went on to lambast the Bank of England's quantitative easing programme for allowing the asset-rich to get even richer (without, of course, doing anything about it). This path provided answers to Corbynism's analysis of what is wrong in Britain in a way that promised to keep the right in power and the ruling class largely unscathed.

The combination of revolts against the 2010–16 settlement quickly proved too great for May to handle. But Johnson took the same course, with greater success.

Johnsonism

Much of the left has been fighting the last war, wanting to fit Johnson into a hard-right, pro-austerity Conservative mould that fails to acknowledge his novelty as a 'Brexity Hezza'. This is Johnson's self-description to his cabinet. Hezza refers to Michael Heseltine, internal opponent of Margaret Thatcher and later deputy prime minister under John Major, who as secretary of state for trade and industry famously said he would intervene in the British economy 'before breakfast, dinner and tea'.

We have to recognise that the Conservatives are one of the most successful political parties in the world. That success – they have been in government for sixty-eight of the last hundred years – rests on a capacity for reinvention. A Tory government took Britain into the European Community in 1972 and another took us out of the European Union in 2020. Ten years ago, a Conservative prime minister preached the gospel of austerity; today, Boris Johnson is anathematised by part of the right as a big-spending heretic.

Despite their interest in propping up the social order, the Conservatives can act as changemakers when necessary. As Tancredi put it in Giuseppe Tomasi di Lampedusa's 1958 novel *The Leopard*, sometimes everything must change for everything to remain the same.[3]

While being tightly bound into the capitalist class through party donors, connections and backgrounds, the Conservatives enjoy freer rein than many equivalent establishment centre-right parties around the world. The Conservatives spent £16 million on the 2019 snap election campaign. By contrast, the 2020 US presidential and congressional elections saw candidates spend a total of $14 billion. The relative cheapness of UK politics provides the Conservative Party with more autonomy with regard to its class bloc, rather than just being directed by those sectors with the deepest pockets. This situation can allow outsized influence to small fractions of capital – such as the volatility-junkie hedge funds' during the Brexit process – but it can also provide the party with much needed room for manoeuvre in times of crisis, when its class bloc requires leadership.

After the 2016 Leave vote, capital accepted that Britain would leave the EU. But in the manner of Tancredi, it wanted a deal that left things fundamentally the same. The Confederation of British Industry was happy to criticise Theresa May's negotiations up until the point they yielded a deal, which it then swung behind, lobbying the Labour opposition to support it. The withdrawal agreement became hopelessly stuck, however, and the governing Conservatives thrown into disarray, not least by the vehemence of the backbench European Research Group caucus. The logjam resembled Marx's description of the French Second Republic on the eve of Louis-Napoléon Bonaparte's 1851 coup d'état,

By splitting up into its hostile factions, the party of Order had long ago lost its independent parliamentary majority. It now showed that there was no longer any parliamentary majority at all. The National Assembly had become incapable of transacting business. Its atomic constituents were no longer held together by any cohesive force; it had used up its last supply of breath. It was dead.[4]

What's more, support for the Conservative and Labour parties had dropped off a cliff.[5] At such junctures, it is sometimes possible for a third figure to enter the fray and shake the system up.[6] That's precisely what Boris Johnson did, playing a role akin to Napoleon III. Emerging from the sidelines, Johnson seized control of the paralysed situation.

The Vote Leave operation that reunited under Johnson's premiership understood that there was a deal to be done with the European Commission. But it would go to the wire, and the other side had to believe that Johnson's stance was more than brinkmanship. The prime minister would play the Nixon 'mad man' role.[7] As the threat of no deal ramped up, capital and the parts of the state over which it has most purchase joined with the overwhelmingly pro-Remain professional managerial classes to attempt an anti-democratic stitch-up. Labelled by its supporters a 'government of national unity', it would have removed both Johnson and Corbyn from their positions.[8] There were real attempts to mount a technocratic coup of the sort Italians are painfully familiar with. Corbyn resisted, but at a cost. The People's Vote campaign took effective control of the Labour whip's office, Corbyn's team was split by an attempt to install Baron Bob Kerslake – former head of the civil service and a People's Vote backer – to head up his operation, and the front bench pivoted to advocating a second referendum in any circumstance. Johnson's team meanwhile doubled down, with establishment resistance reinforcing their narrative to both the British people and the EU. Brexit would happen come what may, despite the would-be saboteurs. Pearl-clutching by the liberal establishment gifted this Old Etonian the opportunity to side with the people against a section of the metropolitan elite.

Labour strategists were deeply divided about how to frame Johnson. A pro-Remain, in-the-national-interest school of thought wanted to avoid 'making this a class/money thing' and instead to attack Johnson's competence and personal probity, on the basis that 'he doesn't care about Britain, he only cares about himself. He is dangerously incompetent and would be a disaster for this country.' An alternative left-populist, respect-the-referendum approach wished to portray Johnson as 'the bankers' best friend and biggest defender', pointing out that during the Tory leadership election his top fiscal priority had been a tax cut for higher earners.[9] Labour's confusion rumbled through to polling day, 12 December 2019.

Heading a party that had been in power for nine years and had sunk to 25 per cent in the polls, Johnson drew substantial dividing lines not only against the Corbyn opposition but also his two predecessors as Tory prime minister, Cameron and May. Unlike them, his would be the government that could both 'get Brexit done' and end austerity.[10] Having won the 2019 general election, Johnson continued to pose as an agent of change, invoking the pandemic as impetus for a (private sector–led) New

Jerusalem akin to the plans for post-war reconstruction developed under Winston Churchill and Clement Attlee from 1942.[11] His 2021 speech to the Conservative Party conference criticised 'decades of drift and dither' in a way that Starmer would baulk at, for its implicit impugning of the New Labour governments of Tony Blair and Gordon Brown. Sounding almost like John McDonnell, he described an 'old broken model: with low wages, low growth, low skills and low productivity'. Of course he swerved the left-wing explanation – the increased wealth and power of the few – and instead blamed 'uncontrolled immigration'. In place of this moribund system, Johnson promised 'a high wage, high skill, high productivity and yes, thereby low tax economy . . . in which everyone can take pride in their work and in the quality of their work'. This new economy was, he claimed, 'the change that people voted for in 2016' and had 'voted for again powerfully in 2019'.

The biggest transformation his leadership brought lies in its presentation of the state. Cameron and George Osborne stood for a shrinking state: fewer services and lower taxes combined with some social liberalism, such as equal marriage. Johnson, on the other hand, argues for a more active one: infrastructure projects and (to the extent that the Treasury and his party allow it) higher all-round government spending; free ports and zero-tax enterprise zones to attract economic activity to left-behind areas; and anti-refugee patrol ships in the Channel. The policies on offer are not materially sufficient to achieve their stated objectives – howls from the austerity-loving libertarian right over emergency pandemic outlays make the government's relatively modest non-Covid spending increases seem more dramatic than they are – but they tell a significant story, especially for Johnson's target audience: voters who don't pay much attention to politics between elections. Gestures not substance is Johnson's speciality.[12]

The media's love of spectacle makes it easy for the Conservatives to trade in right-wing culture wars, not just to distract from their failings but also to secure non-material benefits – what David Roediger calls 'the wages of whiteness' – for an electorally significant portion of the population.[13] Home Secretary Priti Patel's bogus claim that 'certain ethnicities' were partially responsible for the UK's high Covid death rate stoked divisions.[14] The feint has worked so far: 58 per cent held the public responsible for deaths during the second wave; just 28 per cent viewed them as more the government's fault.[15] The statue of Winston Churchill in Parliament Square has become a favoured prop for similar misdirection. The police were allegedly instructed to 'protect Churchill at all costs' during an action at Parliament Square on 14 March 2021 in the backlash from the violent policing of the Sarah Everard vigil on Clapham Common.[16] The absence of threat to the statue was insignificant; the ring of high-vis officers surrounded by protestors made for a compelling image of besieged patriotism.

Limits to right populism

At its strongest, Johnsonism in its 2019 vintage was a hegemonic project to remodel the political terrain and re-establish mass support for a superficially changed system. It is a juggling trick, protecting the status quo at the same time as benefiting from popular frustration with it.[17] He rode to power on a particular right-populist strategy of bringing together different electoral blocs – and their sometimes competing needs and views of the world – into a winning coalition. Much of this approach was developed by the former Vote Leave strategist Dominic Cummings, rather than by Johnson himself, several of whose historic political instincts run counter to it.[18]

But long-term Conservative ascendancy is not a foregone conclusion, despite the supineness of the official opposition. While Johnson has carried out some urgent repairs to the surface structure of ruling-class hegemony – with Labour under Starmer offering little more than a different team to achieve the same end – beyond that, Conservative options narrow. He seems aware that to maintain mass consent in the longer run, the Tories will have to alter Britain's political economy meaningfully so that it serves a wider pool of people. Thatcher did so by expanding home and share ownership as compensation for the demise of manufacturing. Home ownership rose from 55 per cent to 67 per cent of the population between 1980 and the time she left office. These weren't mere shifts at the level of political discourse, but presented material changes to people's lives.

Today, sectors such as construction and haulage have experienced significant wage increases because of the end of free movement from the EU and Covid-related supply chain challenges, but the Office for Budget Responsibility estimates that average wages in Britain will still be below 2008 levels in 2026. Inflation and rising energy costs put firm downward pressure on living standards. To level up parts of the country that have faced forty-plus years of industrial decline and underinvestment would entail shifting significant resources away from the control of asset prices and towards fixed capital investment in the North and Midlands; it cannot be achieved with a few relatively minor funding pots. Expanding home ownership – rightly seen by conservatives around the world as the *sine qua non* of social peace – requires making housing more affordable. But the Conservatives can't share the anaemic rewards of economic activity without confronting capital; nor can they substantially broaden the class of asset-owning mini-capitalists, as Thatcher did, without cutting against the interests of the most numerous base of Conservative voters – smallholders of capital – through their homes and pension pots.

Without the ballast of his Vote Leave team, most of whom, including Cummings, soon left Number 10, Johnson struggled to maintain a hegemonic course in the face of greater internal party resistance.[19] Increased government spending and Covid-19 restrictions enraged small-state Tory MPs and their think-tank outriders. Right-wing populism brought Johnson success, but the Conservatives are not won over to it ideologically. They like the right-wing elements but baulk at the populism. Significant sections of his party don't like the tools he used – and at the first sign of trouble, jitters emerged.

Backbenchers and the Tory press began to grumble noisily after Johnson's mishandling of the Owen Paterson lobbying scandal of autumn 2021. They were furious after Johnson tried to get ahead of the problem by banning MPs from holding certain types of second jobs. Then came the revelations of a series of restriction-defying after-work parties in Downing Street.[20] The 'partygate' scandal soon cost Johnson several of his top team, popularity, two seats in Parliament and support among his MPs, some of whom began trying to replace him as leader.[21] With the drip-drip of media and political pressure growing and the campaign to remove Johnson stoked by former staffers, including

Dominic Cummings. Johnson, it seemed, had only one strategy: to play for time.

When, on 24 February, Russian president Vladimir Putin ordered the invasion of Ukraine, the British media-political class engaged in a screeching change of direction in its attention. The death, destruction and displacement caused by Russia's brutal invasion of its neighbour – and the British establishment's selective moral posturing, by contrast to the UK's support for Saudi–UAE devastation of Yemen – offered Johnson a reprieve. Details of fixed penalty notices began to arrive in April, but carried less immediate media weight.[22] Why after more than 150,000 Covid-19 deaths, the biggest economic downturn among rich economies, and corruption in government contracts was it something so relatively trivial as 'partygate' that threatened to bring an end to his time in office? The sheer hypocrisy of those in power – flouting the rules the rest of the country patiently abided by at great personal and collective cost – is partly behind the popular anger. But it's not a sufficient explanation. To understand why this scandal cut through so dramatically, we need to look to the media. Stoked by a section of the Conservative Party, the billionaire-owned Tory press went hell-for-leather on a story that started in the Starmer-supporting *Mirror*. That's because the scandal opened the floodgates to an opportunist desire among some Conservative MPs and right-wing editors to shift to a 'living with Covid' strategy of zero restrictions and government support and turn off the spending taps more generally. The immense pressure on Johnson had its desired effect: the UK scrapped its Covid restrictions, in spite of hundreds still dying every day, and the March 2022 spring statement showed that talk of high wages and big spending was to be junked in favour of fiscal austerity. In January 2022, Downing Street launched 'operation red meat', a further series of right-wing policies designed to buttress the prime minister's right flank. The government, for example, has maintained its ban on on-shore wind despite Johnson's previous claim that he wanted the UK to become 'the Saudi Arabia of wind'.

The extent of the present social-ecological crisis limits the Conservatives' ability to achieve a comprehensive settlement to it. And while Johnson's luck and flexibility with both the truth and policy have, at time of writing, helped keep him in post, his party's capacity to pursue a hegemonic 'people's government' approach to the overlapping crises that define our current period is now reduced.

Loyal opposition

Keir Starmer won the Labour Party leadership vacated by Corbyn on a platform combining the bulk of his policy advances with a promise of unity and competence. Instead, he has restored Labour to its historic role as the B team for capital, the state and empire, ready for deployment should the preferred political vehicle, the Tories, run into difficulties. As Rory Scothorne has argued, he offers a 'loyal opposition, where the price of the adjective is the meaning of the noun'.[23] Content to play second fiddle to the Conservatives, his strategy for victory scarcely extends beyond praying for the first violin to break a finger.

It is a recognisable Labour position. The party did not adopt a consistent socialist strategy even when it was socialist-led. Wedded to the pageantry and protocols of

Westminster, most Labour politicians find comfort in speaking in terms of the 'national interest' and arguing that Labour, rather than the Conservative Party, is best placed to safeguard it. This approach structures Labour's political metanarrative: its parliamentary team is made up of good managers with good values, whereas the Tories are bad managers with bad values. The party does not, as a rule, critique the capitalist system as such, nor its elite beneficiaries. Instead, it seeks to undermine the public's trust in the Conservatives' ability to manage the system effectively, while simultaneously building trust in Labour's ability to do the same. In foreign affairs, the instinct of most Labour MPs is to tuck in behind the government or even outflank it from the right. Despite the popularity of his anti-war politics among the public, Corbyn could only rely on limited support even within the left of the party.[24]

But there is a thinness to Starmer's politics that is without recent precedent. Despite their wildly different politics, one thing united his four predecessors as Labour leader: they all had an idea of the society they were trying to build. Blair and Brown embraced mild compensatory redistribution alongside financialisation and the globalisation of commodity production, and coupled more funding for public services with extending market processes into their deeper recesses. Miliband initially talked tough about tackling 'predatory' and 'rip-off' forms of capitalism. Corbyn stood for left-wing social democracy and anti-imperialism. Starmer's position, by contrast, is a morass of focus-group platitudes and fence-sitting. Where the party has produced solid, progressive policy announcements, such as on workers' rights or climate change, Starmer has either reframed them in his dull, pro-business, national-interest comfort zone, or failed to champion them at all.[25]

Pressed by Piers Morgan to name his top three priorities in a long ITV interview, Starmer replied with a list of bromides impossible to disagree with and therefore without meaning: 'a first-class education for every child. Second thing, to make sure our economy deals with insecurity and inequality. A third thing is to put real dignity into older age.' Starmer's team was apparently delighted, despite the interview compounding the problem that most people have no idea what he stands for. The focus groups painfully tell them so.

The most telling criticism of the 13,000-word pamphlet for the Fabian Society commissioned from Tony Blair's former speechwriter Philip Collins, published under Starmer's name on the eve of the 2021 party conference, came from Theresa May's former chief of staff Gavin Barwell. He tweeted his agreement with eight of Starmer's 'ten principles' and added that he also partially agreed with the other two. How could he not? Barwell found them 'so bland that they don't tell us anything useful about what he would do if he became prime minister'. Despite being treated with kid gloves by the media, by the spring of 2021 Starmer's personal ratings were about as poor as Jeremy Corbyn's after four years of extreme vilification. By the autumn, more 2019 Labour voters wanted Starmer to resign as leader than to stay in the role.[26] Only Conservative missteps then offered a reprieve from the electorate. 'Tories do not fear Keir', cautions Anne McElvoy of the *Economist*, 'and until they have reason to do so, Labour's paper gains and more positive polling will remain unconsolidated.'[27]

Clearly, the Labour right spent its time in the wilderness planning how to take back the party and never lose it again, but it's hard to find any evidence of fresh political thinking. While Corbyn led the party, practically no policy proposals emerged from the Labour right, despite their well-funded offices and 'shadow' shadow front bench. When deputy leader Tom Watson set up the Future Britain group, an alliance of Blairites and Brownites in Parliament, following the defection of a few pro-corporate Labour MPs to the Independent Group, he claimed it would develop new policies for the party. None were forthcoming. Since the November 2021 reshuffle of Starmer's top team that removed the soft left, the might of the Labour right's policy thinking should have been on full display.[28] But they are yet to propose a single signature policy. Blair and Brown, remember, were hardly short of big ideas, eye-catching announcements and dividing-line policies. The poverty of ideas among the current right is remarkable.

The attack on the left

Starmer's significance lies elsewhere: he has grasped the opportunity to change the Labour Party with both hands. Initially, the Labour left was unsure how to respond to his election as leader, but the idea of hugging him close and trying to hold him to his Corbyn-lite ten pledges quickly became untenable. Labour's rapid transformation – from a party that put taxing the rich centre-stage to one that opposed increases to corporation tax by a Conservative chancellor – has been dismaying and disorientating. Starmer has effectively kicked his predecessor out of the party, set right-wing officials loose to harry the grassroots left and sought to sever ties between the parliamentary and the extra-parliamentary left.[29] Backed by a strong majority on the National Executive Committee, he appointed David Evans – a Millbank veteran from the Blair years – to head up the party machine as general secretary.[30] Evans has forced through a rapid counterrevolution to Corbyn's limited changes to Labour structures, processes and personnel. He has scrapped the Community Organising Unit, provided an exit for the vast majority of remaining left-wing staffers through a voluntary redundancy scheme, and is overseeing a dramatic increase in disciplinary cases against members and local party branches. Evans's restructure of the party machine, under the rubric 'organise to win', can be readily ridiculed – his paper includes such Brentian management speak as suggesting staff engage in 'agile ceremonies' and adopt a 'product mindset' – but its results are deadly serious.

Under this bureaucratic authoritarianism, the Labour apparatus won't organise to change society; instead it shuts down activists who wish to. The party is haemorrhaging members, down by at least a third (200,000) since Starmer became leader. Empty suits and corporate lobbyists are once again more at home in the party than trade unionists, environmentalists and anti-racists. In this context, 'stay and fight' sounds to many members perilously close to 'stay, fight and lose'.

The left is understandably reeling from the near-constant attacks by the Labour bureaucracy and outrages from the front bench. The physical and mental toll that the years of the Corbyn project took on many of the left's leaders and activists must be acknowledged. But the truth is that resistance to Starmer has lacked focus and organisation. The Socialist Campaign Group, which represents the Labour left in Parliament, is less than the sum of its parts.[31] It has yet to set up an effective shadow operation of the sort mounted by the Labour right and stop-Brexit enthusiasts when Corbyn was in charge. Several of its members have undertaken creditable initiatives, but they have not registered in popular consciousness, and the SCG hasn't provided enough counterweight either to slow the rightward drift or to keep members from leaving.

Momentum, the organisation set up out of the first Corbyn leadership campaign, has also struggled in the new era, losing members as activists quit the party. This despite a new leadership, a decent strategy paper which calls for the group to act as a 'bridge between extra-Party struggle and Labour' and a range of positive activities. It remains by some distance the grassroots Labour group with the greatest support, capacity and potential, but does not enjoy a monopoly on activists' loyalties. Sections of the left became alienated during the Corbyn years because of disagreements over internal democracy and the approach to antisemitism and parliamentary selections. Some have thrown themselves into other organisations, none of which appear to have the authority or broad appeal to unite the left within the party, let alone project out into the country. The tendency is towards disunity rather than coordination.[32]

Vulnerabilities of the Labour right

The Labour right has always predominated within the Parliamentary Labour Party – broadly defined, it has almost 80 per cent of MPs – and uses its control of the NEC and party apparatus, as well as its proximity to sections of the state and the media, to strike at the left.[33] But it isn't unassailable. The two main social constituencies it represents are shrinking. The old right, associated with the Labour First faction, represents a working-class, trade union and steadfastly revisionist social-democratic tradition. Based in the manufacturing industries that boomed in the three decades after the Second World War, it stands for an authentic labourism, a desire to improve the lot of working-class people within the parameters of the capitalist framework.[34] It was, therefore, firmly in support of the extra-economic elements that maintained the social order: the monarchy, the empire and the Cold War. In the 1950s through to the 1970s, this labourist tradition represented a substantial section of the working class who had a stake in the system and could see that stake expanding over time. Today, with the decline of manufacturing, stagnant or declining real wages and the demise of the institutions of the social-democratic social contract, this constituency has shrunk dramatically.

The new right, associated with the Progress faction, represents a professional-managerial class that came to dominate Labour in the 1990s and 2000s. Thatcher's financialisation of Britain's political economy expanded a class of salaried people who formally service other businesses through finance, legal advice, public affairs, advertising and management consultancy. A substantial section of this group animated the new-right elements of New Labour, hence its obsession with the City, creative industries and outsourcing. While the new right still enjoys close ties with the liberal end of the media, other demographic and economic changes mean that a substantial part of the social base it represented calls for different politics. Those that entered the salaried professions prior to the New Labour government have enjoyed substantial financial success. They began their careers at a time when fewer graduates meant less competition, and they were likely able to buy their homes before house prices and wage growth were entirely decoupled, the former surging ahead in the late 1990s. But their younger counterparts now enter professional life in a cohort where nearly half are graduates and housing is unaffordable. The children of the section of society who drove the New Labour revolution now find themselves well to the left of today's bland pro-corporate new-right Labour politics, animated instead by issues of climate change, unaffordable housing and inequality across lines of wealth, race and gender.

This sociological shift is part of the reason for the increased popularity of socialist measures. The recent examples of Labour success come from the left of the party, not its right. The Labour left holds national government in Wales and local government in a number of towns and cities including the greater Newcastle region, Preston, Salford, Worthing and North Ayrshire. In each case, they are led by members who supported Corbyn as Labour Party leader. First Minister Mark Drakeford, Mayor Jamie Driscoll, and council leaders Matthew Brown and Paul Dennett are being rewarded at the ballot box for pursuing green, progressive, social-democratic policies. Drakeford, who advanced Welsh Labour in the 2021 Senedd elections, has a governing programme in alliance with Plaid Cymru that includes expanding free childcare and free school meals, a national care service, rent controls and a publicly owned energy company. In Manchester, meanwhile, Andy Burnham continues to reposition himself more to the left, challenging both the government and the Labour establishment and promoting public ownership. It may be a cost-free routine to pull off for a metropolitan mayor with few formal powers, but the point still stands: Starmer only became leader because a majority of Labour members thought he would be that sort of Labour leader. The overwhelming majority of Labour members and trade unionists – as well as the public – support the progressive ten pledges on which Starmer ran for the leadership. It is not just embarrassing for Starmer to have dumped them so unceremoniously, but delegitimising too.

Today, Labour's right is better at getting its way within the party than appealing to the country. Its undoubted factional success rests on shaky ground. Starmer was elected to create a Corbynism-lite that could win a general election. His backers want him to be 'both Kinnock and Blair', but in reality they know that he is no Blair.[35] Their plan is for him to hand over to their new Blair – perhaps Wes Streeting or Bridget Phillipson – having made enough changes to the party to give this successor free rein, with the left either purged or radically neutralised. But for this succession planning to be secure, the Labour right needs either a more pliable party membership, a compelling candidate or a compelling agenda. None seem forthcoming.

In the following chapter I argue that there is a large base of potential activists and an even larger section of the population available for mobilisation, but at present no central switching room to coordinate them. The leader of the opposition is in thrall to median-voter theory and the shrinking constituency of the Labour right. The left's malaise at national level resides, then, in a crisis of political representation. It's a problem, but also an opportunity to try something new.

3

Our Bloc

For years, many on the left either consoled themselves with or despaired of Britain's supposed conservatism. We no longer have that excuse for failure. The hegemony of Westminster's Tweedledum and Tweedledee is more apparent than real. The material conditions that could power a progressive advance are present – if anything, they have strengthened. Millions of workers – particularly younger workers – are locked out of the Thatcherite–New Labour compact of asset-based capitalism. The legacy of the Corbyn project has been a general leftward shift in public attitudes. Support for higher public spending rose from almost half the population in 2016 to over three-fifths after the 2017 general election campaign.[1] Support for rail renationalisation increased by 6 percentage points to 64 per cent between that election and its sequel in 2019. The popularity of other renationalisations increased in step.[2]

Forceful arguments change minds and crowd out those of opponents. Few today would defend the existing economic model in its entirety or attempt to deny the urgency of the climate crisis. The common sense about these issues, and the solutions to them, lean in a progressive direction. Upon this plinth progressive forces and left politics could stand.

But how do we turn this potential into a reality with sufficient collective strength to transform Britain's political, social and ecological landscape? Ploughing on in Labour in the way we are, with little plan to win it back or overhaul it, is unlikely to get us very far. Nor would the formation of a new fringe party by a small number of MPs and activists be of any help to us. The first-past-the-post system raises significant barriers to entering Westminster politics.[3] The recently formed Northern Independence Party and the Breakthrough Party both have a lively online presence and propose radical policies, and they have formed a People's Alliance of the Left with two pre-Corbyn-era left parties, Left Unity and the Trade Union and Socialist Coalition. But neither of them, alone or in alliance, has come close to winning a council seat or retaining a parliamentary by-election deposit. For its part, the Green Party has made no effort to court Corbyn-era activists. It has gained some former Labour voters but continues to play a marginal role in British political life.

No new party can flourish without being connected to substantial organised social forces, such as the trade unions. A purely electoral – and mainly online – force won't have the social weight to change things. Calls for an instant breakaway from Labour often take the form of begging Corbyn and other socialist Labour MPs to set up their own shop. But without the level of social and political organisation that would be needed to surpass Labour in one, or at most two electoral cycles, they would likely be walking into political oblivion. Forming a minor left party would also hinder movement-building, sucking in activism and energy better invested elsewhere. Despite its media representation as a cult of weirdos, the Corbyn movement's greatest strength was how normal it was. Everyday people were brought into politics with a clear focus on winning power to change lives. Marginality necessarily shifts horizons away from a majoritarian appeal and winning power. Relying on a new party without the vision, strength and structure required to overtake Labour in quick time as the main anti-Tory vehicle would be to accept the sidelining of progressive ideas.

There is another option. Socialist solutions are popular in the UK, but left leaders are rarely heard in the mass media, even after five years of some success in shaping political discourse. Ultimately, to redress this problem, we need strong, well-organised and interconnected movements able to mobilise the mass of the country – *as well as* a political party with the skill to win elections, the will to carry through its policies and sufficient openness to movements to prevent its deradicalisation once in office. We are a long way off those arrangements. But the question of whether Labour or a new left party can be the vehicle for socialist advance puts the cart before the horse. Instead, we should set our sights on bolstering progressive forces and knitting them together, so that we can determine the electoral question from a position of greater strength.

The idea of a federation of movements was on the glimmering horizon of Labour's new left of the 1970s and 1980s.[4] The Corbyn project could have made this a reality, Katrina Forrester argues, but there was never enough bandwidth to pursue such a strategy.[5] One might have hoped that the left-led trade unions would use their organisational heft to cajole the Socialist Campaign Group MPs and grassroots groups into a more coherent formation. But efforts by Len McCluskey to bring together seven Labour-affiliated and left-led trade unions into a formal organisation did not bear fruit. Now we must build such a federation so that we can, down the line, be better prepared to challenge for state power.

Counter-hegemonic struggles

What are progressive social forces? Put simply, they are the movements and organisations needed to mobilise widespread grievances with the ruling order into meaningful popular power: to turn a 'sociological majority' into a 'political majority'.[6] The numerous abuses of capital and the state – degraded environments, exploited workers, marginalised populations – generate a myriad of resistance. They are all counter-hegemonic responses to the failure of the ruling bloc to live up to its promises.[7] During the Corbyn period, many movement activists ploughed their energies into Labour. Since December 2019, on the other hand, large popular constituencies have been politicised by reinvigorated campaigns around the axes of race, gender and class.

The Black Lives Matter (BLM) protests in the summer of 2020 had a profound effect on the British social and political landscape. As a result of the uprising, 60 per cent of eighteen- to twenty-four-year-olds say they have been speaking more about race. The English Premier League adopted the slogan on the back of players' shirts and most players take the knee before kick-off to express their opposition to racism. The ground on which politics sits was shifted, disorientating the Labour leadership. Keir Starmer was also widely criticised for dismissing BLM as just 'a moment' and deriding the movement's demands, but tried to play both sides by taking the knee in a staged photograph in his office. The Conservatives were, of course, more forthright in their opposition, with Priti Patel criticising the England football team for 'gesture politics' for taking the knee and defending those that might boo the team while they did it. The attempted hard-right backlash failed as most of the country rejected racism and got firmly behind the England team, which made it to the finals of the European Championship in the summer of 2021. Opinion polls show a plurality of support for BLM UK, whose activists were also prominent in the Kill the Bill protests of spring and summer 2021, organising alongside Sisters Uncut, Extinction Rebellion and a range of other groups – demonstrations which drew a young, diverse and militant crowd.[8]

Sisters Uncut, a feminist direct-action group founded in 2014 to defend domestic-violence services, led the reaction to police violence at the vigil for Sarah Everard, a young woman who was abducted and murdered by an off-duty police officer in March 2021, channelling public anger.

The Crime Survey for England and Wales suggests a fifth of women have experienced sexual assault. Conviction rates for rape are so low that campaigners have said the crime has effectively been decriminalised. On the first anniversary of the Clapham Common vigil, Sisters Uncut set off 1,000 rape alarms outside Charing Cross police station to protest against police abuse.

Extinction Rebellion was formed in October 2018 in response to the latest IPCC report, and, through eye-catching protests including shutting down Westminster Bridge, demanded that the government first of all tell the truth about the climate emergency. Their actions raised ecological consciousness in the population and drove climate issues onto the political agenda. Unsurprisingly, their success and popularity has led to bipartisan political attacks. The government arrests, criminalises, and criticises activists while the Labour front bench demands anti-oil protests are banned and Shadow Justice Secretary Steve Reed attacks a Conservative official for defending Extinction Rebellion.[9] Fortunately, Extinction Rebellion is not alone in efforts to save the planet from climate collapse. They are joined by a number of other groups in the ecological mix, such as Fridays for Future, direct-action group Just Stop Oil and Green New Deal Rising, a youth group styled after the US Sunrise Movement.

In the labour movement – the largest and best-organised social movement in the UK, and a necessary lynchpin for a wider set of progressive campaigns – there are encouraging signs of growing energy. Forty years of decline have come to an end, with 2017, 2018, 2019 and 2020 all seeing modest increases in total union membership, which now stands at over 6.5 million workers.[10] This change of tide is significant. Over the neoliberal period, inequality rose as union membership fell from a peak of 13 million in 1979. The labour share of national income dropped from almost two-thirds to just over half. These trends are not coincidences. There is a reason Thatcher set out to destroy the unions. Without strong unions, it is impossible durably to advance the interests of the overwhelming majority of workers. During the first year of the pandemic, industries with higher union density faced lower rates of redundancy. Unite fought off a wave of attempts to fire and rehire by major employers such as British Airways, Weetabix, Tesco and Go North West.[11] Already the most active trade union of the past decade, Unite elected Sharon Graham to succeed Len McCluskey as general secretary in August 2021. Graham won her position on a platform of building organised groups of stewards and members across employees in a given sector. The aim is to achieve effective sectoral collective bargaining from below.[12]

Meanwhile, the Communication Workers Union (CWU) has won the largest vote for strike action – 97 per cent on a 76 per cent turnout of 110,000 postal workers – since the introduction of the restrictive 2016 Trade Union Act. After the ballot, Royal Mail's CEO quit and the company ditched its plans to strip back to being just a parcel courier, instead adopting a different growth model that includes shorter working hours for postal workers. Elsewhere the Bakers' Union has brought the Service Employees International Union's 'Fight for $15' campaign from the US to the UK, organising McDonald's workers around the demand for a wage of £15 per hour.[13] The expanding gig economy is host to smaller unions such as Industrial Workers of Great Britain, United Voices of the World and the App Drivers and Couriers Union. Deliveroo and Uber in particular have faced both industrial action and legal challenges.[14] We have also seen shoots of community unionism, where worker demands are linked to community needs. The 2015–16 British Medical Association junior doctors' strikes, a threatened Royal College of Nursing strike, University and College Union industrial action in higher education and Unison's organising among care workers all have traces of this approach.[15]

There's a long way to go to rebuild numbers, breadth, depth and militancy in the union movement. Only around 13 per cent of private sector workers are trade union members, and strikes are still rare by historical standards. The booming 1950s and 1960s, which saw the UK's highest levels of sustained growth alongside falling inequality, lost more than six times as many days to strikes than the period between 1996 and 2019.[16] But recent successes can be built upon. Corbyn and his shadow chancellor John McDonnell revalorised trade unions in public discourse, standing with them in industrial disputes and praising their actions. Under their leadership, the unions moved from being treated as an embarrassment to a key driving force. Over a hundred policies submitted by trade unions were included in Labour's 2017 manifesto.[17] An injection of energy came from below, too, with new activists drawn into political life by the Corbyn project joining trade unions and becoming active in them.

Building a bloc

A movement turn has seen an outflow of activism, energy and skills from Labour into other vital social and industrial activity. We need an entity that can unite the remaining Labour left with movements – an interlocking structure of alliances equipped with a shared secretariat to coordinate between groups, mount campaigns, wield a parliamentary voice and form a pole of attraction in popular struggle. Federated forces are stronger. Our aim should be to form a counter-hegemonic bloc to contest the ruling historic bloc that currently transposes elite interests onto the general interest of society.

A complete left bloc will not be formed in one fell swoop. Instead, it will develop over time, in concentric circles, as trust between groups builds up and formalised cooperation proves its worth. Federation can be pushed from below, by ordinary members. It can also proceed through ad hoc alliances around discrete campaigns, and by means of formal negotiations at leadership level. These routes are not mutually exclusive. Trade unionists can call on their branches and executives to reduce discretionary funding to Labour – as both Unite and the CWU have begun to do – to free up resources for other activities. General secretaries can agree institutional alliances among themselves that would also seek to include other progressive forces. With their labour-movement authority, the allied unions can bring on board the (bulk of the) Socialist Campaign Group of MPs, as well as left Members of the Scottish Parliament and Welsh Senedd. The parliamentarians could contribute some funds for the pooling of resources in a secretariat to handle the media and coordinate among the MPs, setting them up like a shadow opposition, just as the Labour right and continuity-Remain campaigns did under Corbyn's leadership. Members of Momentum and other Labour left organisations – such as the Campaign for Labour Party Democracy, Labour Representation Committee, Compass, Red Labour, Campaign for Socialism in Scotland and Welsh Labour Grassroots in Wales – can promote cross-affiliation, including with left trade unions. Several unions, including the CWU and the Fire Brigades Union, are already affiliated to Momentum, for example. Our bloc wouldn't seek to replace Momentum, but rather would build on it. No other Labour left organisation can mobilise as many people or communicate so effectively.

As we have seen, the labour movement is on the up, but from a very low base. While membership will most likely only surge around major disputes – as happened in the National Education Union during the battle over reopening schools in January 2021 – much can be done to grow membership in our unions outside of these climactic moments.[18] Only about a third of Labour members are in a trade union, despite this technically being a requirement for party membership. This suggests that perhaps around half a million people in and around the left could join a union. The left bloc could run a union drive for current and former Labour members and supporters. That could add to union density and dues and help to anchor Labour's remaining membership in the wider labour movement, at a time when the Labour leadership is turning its head to wealthy donors.

The left bloc could help strengthen campaigns within unions to push them to the left and to take more self-confident positions. The ability to call on a wider range of organisations and voices for campaigns should particularly appeal to Unite, which has led the way through leverage campaigns. These are non-traditional union campaigns that combine direct-action stunts and clever communications with industrial muscle. Leverage is used when a strike is not possible because density is low, the union isn't recognised or for some other reason. The aim is to make life difficult for the employer, find its weak points and exert pressure until it gives in to demands. Graham has set her sights on Amazon, in what could be Unite's first offensive leverage campaign.

From a base in the largest sections of the Labour left, our bloc could radiate further outwards. Unions not affiliated to Labour could join, such as the Bakers', RMT, PSC, IWGB and UVW. In addition to the struggle for better work, there is the struggle for work itself. Unemployment hasn't been a central political issue in the UK for some time, but mass joblessness persists. Beginning under Thatcher, governments have removed many of the economically inactive – such as redundant industrial workers – from the official jobless rate, which was below 5 per cent in the five years prior to the pandemic. The *real* unemployment rate in 2019 was estimated by the OECD and Centre for Cities to be 13 per cent.[19] Unemployment levels are projected to be higher after the pandemic, not even accounting for those who are underemployed or have been pushed out of the labour market altogether. Higher inflation has already led the Bank of England to begin the process of raising interest rates, potentially pushing more people out of work.

Though Unite has a community membership arm that engages with those not in full-time work, unemployed activism is currently negligible. Our bloc could get ahead of the curve by setting up an unemployed workers' movement. Such a movement could campaign for the longer-term goals of full employment, a shorter working week and a citizens' payout from a people's asset manager (the operations of private asset managers are an underexplored area for progressive activism). It could also provide immediate support in the form of mutual aid and cooperatives, and link up with debtors' unions and the inspirational Disabled People Against Cuts (DPAC). Unite Community, Momentum and others within the bloc could join forces to create the basic infrastructure, using their lists and platforms to seek out a membership, while trialling and facilitating forms of mutual support and activism, and acting as a powerful political voice for the unemployed.

Corbyn made bringing community organising to Labour part of his campaign platform in 2016. This effort was eventually rolled out as the Community Organising Unit once Iain McNicol had resigned as general secretary in March 2018 and been replaced by Jennie Formby. Despite obstruction and a clash of political cultures with the more traditional Labour-right staff in the party's regional offices, the COU was successful. The most diverse team in the Labour Party, its twenty organisers fanned out across key seats around the country. With the constant threat of an early election hanging over party staff and the need to demonstrate the immediate electoral benefits of community organising, the unit's greatest achievements lay in mobilisation, rather than deep organising. The results of the 2019 election show the approach was beginning to bear fruit: in seats with a community organiser, the swing against Labour was two points less than the national swing.[20] While the need for community organising is relatively well understood on the left, even fashionable, no organisation has filled the hole left by Labour's scrapping of the unit in 2020. If the left bloc were to be able to pool resources effectively, it could fill that gap, hiring organisers who could then train an army of activists around the country.

Our bloc would also need to expand out to other movements and struggles that animate our age. Some may join readily, thanks to longstanding ties with major figures and organisations on the Labour left. Corbyn, for example, is particularly close to Stop the War and the Palestine Solidarity Campaign, while McDonnell is a long-time champion of Disabled People Against Cuts. For others from different political traditions, it may take time and mutual flexibility. Local cooperation between left groups can create the well-spring for formal federation at national level.

Alliances already exist, sometimes bringing together striking and novel formations. The Kill the Bill protests were organised by diverse movements and organisations working together. Another example, is BLM, XR, Unite the Community and the Trades Union Congress (London, East and South-East Region) working together to oppose an expansion of the Edmonton incinerator. They were supported by others, such as Jeremy Corbyn and his Peace and Justice Project.

The Make Amazon Pay campaign offers a further encouraging global example. It has brought together more than seventy organisations, including almost all the trade unions active in Amazon, as well as environmental and tax justice groups, to stage global days of strikes and protests.[21] These actions have connected workers throughout the Amazon supply chain – dockers, factory workers, truckers, warehouse workers, delivery drivers, call centre workers, office staff, tech workers. They have joined their diverse labour issues with calls for climate action, racial justice, indigenous rights, privacy, data autonomy, consumer rights, consideration for small business and non-militarisation. These demands, synthesised by the campaign into twenty-five common agenda items, are heard by Amazon at many levels: from citizens, consumers, workers and their unions, and politicians – hundreds of whom, from dozens of countries, are members of the Parliamentary Alliance to Make Amazon Pay. This situation results in a many-versus-one effect, with combined issues, geographies and levels focusing collective resistance against a common opponent. In the

UK, the campaign brings together GMB, Unite, Momentum and War on Want. Most encouragingly, the global day of action on Black Friday, 26 November 2021, was also supported by Extinction Rebellion, which blockaded Amazon warehouses in solidarity with the global movement, grabbing further media attention.

To keep environmentalists, workers, and other campaigners under the same banner will need more than a promise of decarbonisation through good, green, unionised jobs. We will need to find a way, for example, of framing core demands for housing – such as rent controls and new (eco-friendly) social homes. The renters' movement could also be grown quickly as part of the left bloc. Tenants' unions currently cover a small fraction of the UK's 14.5 million working-age renters, who pay landlords over £50 billion a year in rent – about a third of their combined annual earnings.[22]

While the issue of housing has risen in political salience, and the correlation between housing tenure and voting is particularly strong, tenants' demands struggle to gain national prominence. We could change that with a combination of spectacle, organising and resistance. Tenants' demands, such as an end to no-fault evictions, voting on redevelopments and rent controls, could be brought to the forefront of the national conversation through a well-chosen target and campaign. On threat of eviction or rent hike, tenants could take collective action, knowing they were backed up by the entirety of the left bloc. This type of spectacle would force tenants' issues and tax justice into the news agenda for a stretch of time. Such prominence could be used to spur on greater sign-ups to tenants' union membership. Momentum activists and others could join Acorn, London Renters Union and other organisations to go door to door, introducing the tenants' union to renters. Trade unions and others with large email databases could encourage their members and supporters who are tenants to join their renters' union. Renters will need the protection of a union and the solidarity across our movements in the coming years as a potential wave of post-pandemic evictions crashes down on thousands of households.

The high-water mark of government attacks on marginalised people and communities has not yet been reached. The Conservatives will lean heavily on such tactics as they fail sufficiently to broaden the material basis for their rule and as Brexit recedes in the back window. One strand of thinking that runs through all Tory Party tendencies is divide and rule, encouraging parts of the working-class majority to kick down rather than punch up. Mimicking the US right, the Conservatives and their allies are pushing back hard against BLM, including by trying to ban it from schools. A right-populist turn was signalled by the December 2020 speech of Liz Truss as women and equalities minister, ending two decades of official liberal consensus; this is coupled with continuing government policies that aggressively target migrants and minorities. Priti Patel has announced a 'regular drumbeat' of deportations and off-shore processing centres, and will continue to stoke fears about refugees crossing the Channel. The well-developed repertoire of migrant baiting – 'go home' vans, hostile environment policies, mediatised raids, border violence, restrictions of rights and services to racialised populations – will likely be embellished further as climate breakdown increases the number of people on the move across the globe. If we are to construct a social majority, the left bloc must defend marginalised communities, be consistent in its anti-racism and unite the majority in a programme for fundamental change.

We would all benefit from greater solidarity between left political and social forces. Questions of disability, for example, have flown under the political radar for too long. Including Disabled People Against Cuts in the formal alliance would not only add serious direct-action skill and experience, but also help to make the social model of disability mainstream throughout the left.[23]

A vehicle for a social majority

Cooperation across institutional lines isn't easy. A degree of friction is inevitable. It took years for Victorian trade unionists to agree upon the creation of a Trades Union Congress, owing to 'a spirit of rivalry' between constituent organisations.[24] We have less time at our disposal. Endlessly debating horizontal versus vertical organisation is to get hung up on a paralysing false dualism, argues Rodrigo Nunes. The point is to 'adopt tactics and practices not for the sake of sustaining an identity but because they look like they might work'.[25] Ours would be a federated organisation where there is no compulsion on members of the alliance. It would live by demonstrating the success of its model of federated forces and pooled resources. That means achieving visibly greater efficacy in campaigns, communications, mobilising and organising.

This is where a properly resourced and empowered secretariat, staffed by some of the most capable organisers and communicators from across our movements, would be pivotal. The secretariat would be charged with coordinating across the federated forces, advancing collective campaigns and interests and securing maximum attention for progressive positions. It could make sure all our forces are on the pitch at the best time and in the best formation to grow, improve lives and advance towards our strategic horizon. With a well-resourced and empowered team, the combined weight of progressive assets – people, platforms, organisations – could be brought to bear in a focused way on the campaigns and issues of the day. On a practical level, the secretariat would run a shared grid or diary of activities, collectively agreed, extending the coordination, reach and impact of each action. Crucially, it would encourage the cross-fertilisation of issues and campaigns to bring greater unity to progressive forces. The aim is to learn to articulate our struggles together under shared banners, without folding one entirely into the other.

With good coordination and proper resourcing, the left bloc would make movement voices louder and our organising more effective. Both campaigns by individual organisations and wider national campaigns would gain from coordination and political coherence. With left MPs, trade unions and members all working together – and buttressed by progressive movements outside Labour – the Labour left would have a much greater ability to act within the party. Rather than treat the left as a punching bag, the party leadership would know the left could strike back. Our bloc would form a pole of attraction for Labour members, giving them a clear alternative position to that of the leadership on issues of the day. It would keep alive the hope for socialist advance through the party where currently there is none, and form the viable organisational basis for an alternative political path if that becomes required. We can't predict the future, of course. But in most conceivable eventualities, the *our bloc* strategy makes our movements stronger and more united, enlarges our ability to act in society and increases the likelihood of creating a movement-party capable of winning elections, taking power and overturning the established order. It's our best chance to win.

4

Movement Populism

To build power, and to lend coherence across our federated forces, we need a banner that all could hold aloft. What message might it carry? The most effective political communications pre-empt an opponent's actions, turn their strengths into weaknesses, and one's own weaknesses into strengths. Hillary Clinton's huge sway over the donor class was among her greatest assets heading into the 2016 Democratic primary race. Bernie Sanders nearly upset the odds by turning that logic on its head, framing his campaign as a political revolution funded by small-dollar donations.[1] In the UK, Corbyn at his best successfully repurposed attacks from the ruling bloc, on one occasion agreeing that investment bank Morgan Stanley was right to call Labour a 'threat', because it wanted to transform a 'damaging and failed system that's rigged for the few'.

A left bloc could learn from such experiences. Several party-based revolts against neoliberalism in the Global North over the past decade adopted elements of left populism, bringing together diverse demands and resistance to different oppressions into a single line of antagonism between an expansive *us* – disparate social forces collected under one banner – and a constrained *them*, the ruling powers.[2] In an age when trust in the status quo is low and those in charge are struggling to reassert a stable hegemony, the right is drawing populist and purportedly anti-systemic divisions of its own choosing.[3] It is not enough for the left to offer voters 'real change' without giving them a strong sense of their own connectedness against a common adversary. Where new hegemonic projects are afoot, as Ernesto Laclau and Chantal Mouffe argue, 'a left alternative can *only* consist of the construction of a different system of equivalents, which establishes social division on a new basis'.[4] To defeat powerful right-wing populism, we will need to be even sharper, with clearer, more majoritarian divides, attracting attention through controversy.[5]

Our story must be distinct from and better than theirs. Mouffe acknowledges that left populism does not offer 'a fully fledged political programme'.[6] It requires a political agent – identity unspecified – to bring us together under a single banner. The UK no longer has a political party to perform that function. Movements, rather than a political party, will have to shoulder the burden. The conjuncture invites an expansion of left populism, not its rejection. I call this adaptation *movement populism*. It maintains the populist core of Mouffe's theory: a cohesion of diverse demands and struggles into a single political antagonism; a majoritarian tilt at state power; and use of controversial, attention-grabbing tactics. In an attention economy, movements can grab attention and alter public attitudes through spectacular actions. A left bloc can shape the wider narrative within which British politics sits.

A red-green banner

The strategy of assimilating the demands of diverse constituencies under one political banner is not new. The Bolsheviks successfully expressed the common interests of workers, peasants and soldiers in 1917 with their slogan 'bread, land and peace'. Today, Mouffe champions the Green Democratic Revolution, a visualisation of ecological transition which connects 'defence of the environment with the manifold democratic struggles against different forms of inequality'. An umbrella term, it leans towards anti-capitalism in a non-sectarian spirit. Mouffe enfolds within it the Green New Deal of Alexandria Ocasio-Cortez and the Sunrise Movement in the US and Green Industrial Revolution championed by Labour under Corbyn.[7] I would settle on the Green New Deal as the most effective slogan for a left bloc in this time of climate breakdown, despite *new deal* having greater historical resonance in the US than in the UK. 'Green New Deal' makes for a simple chant. It already has purchase on the international left, and has partly acquired class-conflict significance through AOC's association of it with tax hikes for the rich and big corporations. That said, a Green New Deal formula needs to carry radical democratic meaning too.

We would not be starting from scratch in seeking to federate the labour and ecological movements around a Green New Deal. Veterans of Corbynism are involved throughout the environmental movement. Corbyn himself boasts a long track record as an environmentalist, although he had only made limited advances in the green agenda by the autumn of 2018.[8] The environmental movement then swelled to unprecedented proportions at the end of that year and through 2019, forcing climate breakdown into public consciousness. Labour was porous to movement demands, and produced probably the most developed set of climate, energy and industrial policies in the Global North.[9]

The Fire Brigades Union was at the forefront in pushing radical policies through the Labour Party, working with Labour for a Green New Deal and other environmental groups. With the increase in fires caused or intensified by climate breakdown, the union's general secretary Matt Wrack declared the climate crisis an industrial issue for his members. The Corbyn project encouraged further coordination between labour groups and the environmental movement. Corbyn and Shadow Business Secretary Rebecca Long-Bailey toured the country throughout 2019, holding consultation meetings with unions, environmentalists, community groups and businesses to develop their manifesto policies. Even GMB, which has had a more fractious relationship with environmental groups, set aside ill feeling to coordinate with Extinction Rebellion in Make Amazon Pay's November 2021 actions.

We have already seen how climate-change campaigners are leading the way by building alliances with other groups. They are also using dramatic spectacle to gain attention. A left bloc could be the logical extension of these impressive practices. With COP26 a dismal failure, and the political path increasingly closed off, more radical action is being discussed and taken by sections of the environmental movement.[10] This more radical turn has begun to show itself in the UK. Some environmentalist tactics have been misguided, such as efforts in October 2019 to prevent predominantly working-class east Londoners from commuting, or the actions by Insulate Britain, an XR offshoot, to shut down major motorways, including the M25 ring road around London, without adequate preparation of public opinion.[11] In the round, however, direct action has turbocharged the environmental movement. Without the disruption caused by Extinction Rebellion, the UK branch of Fridays for Future would be written off as the apolitical actions of schoolchildren.[12]

By placing the Green New Deal at the centre of a left bloc strategy for the 2020s, the ecology movement would rightly take up a central position, grow and orientate itself politically. There is a tendency among some environmentalists – including within XR – to think of themselves as 'beyond politics', or to flop into middle-class liberalism when engaging with electoral politics, as in Germany.[13] An injection of majoritarian class politics will help climate-change campaigners build more durable mass backing. They will need it. With the governments of the world failing to prevent or plan for the climate collapse the scientific projections imply – vast unliveable swathes of earth, extreme natural disasters, unprecedented levels of migration and insufficient energy and food to sustain our population – a wave of radical direct action is assured. Activists will run up against attempts by state authorities to criminalise as much dissent as possible.[14] The wider left will have to be vocal in support of the environmental movement and skilled at defeating its detractors in the court of public opinion as well as law. The negative response from liberals and conservatives was swift and effective when Extinction Rebellion blockaded Rupert Murdoch's printing presses in September 2020; much of the left was nowhere to be seen. The left bloc can help us do better.

Our Green New Deal programme must tell a bigger political story, and encourage everyone to feel able and willing to contribute. We need to both unite the struggle at the end of the month with the struggle against the end of the world and develop our understanding of *them*: not just the big polluters and City investors, but also dodgy landlords, rip-off bosses, tax cheats and the media barons that prop up this rotten system. If the antagonism between the many and the few isn't written into the code of public understanding of the Green New Deal, the term will be co-opted by the neoliberal centre as a limited programme for managerial reform, like the EU's Green Deal. The Johnson government has already neutralised the Green Industrial Revolution term.[15] Indeed it has a habit of adopting the insufficiently defined slogans of the centre left. 'Build Back Better', for example, is a terrible political slogan for the left. You can tell it is meaningless because nobody would propose its opposite; who wants to build back worse? An array of organisations – the US and UK governments, the World Economic Forum and the United Nations – have all made use of the slogan for exactly that reason. It is marketing speak, not politics.

One approach for the left bloc would be a series of actions that involve different elements of the 'many' targeting different representatives of the 'few'. Big polluters could be targeted through coordinated sit-ins, pickets and teach-ins at the offices of fossil fuel companies or the biggest recipients of fossil fuel subsidies, or through blockades of fossil fuel extraction or processing sites. The principle of such actions should be to deliver a media spectacle by disrupting the activities of our opponents while minimising disruption to the lives of the over-whelming majority of the population, whom we need on our side.[16] Spectacle is created through a shock factor or element of surprise, along with coordination across locat-ions and participants to keep the story moving. For example, experienced climate direct activists could occupy the offices of major oil companies. Fridays for Future and Green New Deal Rising could organise mass pickets of young people and their supporters outside the office build-ings to protect the occupiers. Activist shareholders could call a press conference to issue demands. Trade unionists and Black Lives Matter activists could use the occupied office space to hold televised teach-ins about energy trans-ition and how black and brown communities, both in the UK and around the world, are already experiencing the climate emergency. Momentum could organise a rally nearby, with Socialist Campaign Group speakers to chan-nel demands into the Green New Deal.

Or consider quantitative easing, the greatest single state policy implemented since the financial crisis. The British ruling class victory of the 2010s saw the wealth of the rich-est thousand rise by almost £450 billion, while workers lost around £400 billion in pay.[17] This redistribution from bottom to top was secured through misdirection. Quan-titative easing has seen the Bank of England create almost £1 trillion (over £15,000 for every person in the UK) to buy financial assets. Rather than boosting bank lending to support the real economy, this unparalleled injection of cash into financial markets inflated the wealth of the richest. The policy is a handout of gigantic proportions, yet it rarely features in public debate – in part through woeful report-ing, in part because the policy is purposefully technocratic rather than democratic, decided by a bank insulated from popular scrutiny.[18] Spectacle could bring the issue to the fore. It fits perfectly with the frames provided by 'the many versus the few' and the Green New Deal. And the demand is simple: liquidity could be created by the central bank to finance green investment, as part of a GND, rather than puffing up the asset wealth of those who are already supremely wealthy.[19]

Progressive common sense

Could our communications gain purchase, with a hostile mainstream media against them? It is a good question. But we should remember that the media is a site of struggle, not a monolithic force. It reproduces – but can also change – the established order. Newspapers, although diminished, still set the agenda for more tightly regulated broadcasters. The British print media is often called the Tory press. In reality, it is the oligarchs' press. Ownership has so much congealed that just three companies control 90 per cent of national newspaper circulation. Commercial radio is no more plural, with two companies holding more than two-thirds of licences. In theory, Britain's large public media should help insulate the news we receive from establishment pressure. But Johnson – like Blair before him – has no compunction in using patronage and threats to shape the output of the state broadcaster.[20]

Johnson has appointed Richard Sharp as chair of the BBC. Sharp is a Conservative Party donor and former banker at JP Morgan and Goldman Sachs, where he was Rishi Sunak's boss. He was also an advisor to Boris Johnson as mayor of London. Johnson's team has also placed Robbie

Gibb, Theresa May's director of communications, on the BBC board. Gibb, whose brother was a Conservative minister, had been running the BBC's political output before joining May's team after the 2017 general election. The BBC director general, meanwhile, is Tim Davie, a former Conservative council candidate and vice chair of the Hammersmith Tories. Culture Secretary Nadine Dorries has told the *Daily Telegraph* that she doesn't know if the BBC will still exist in ten years' time, but the corporation should be harmless enough by then.[21]

Theresa May called the 2017 election at perhaps the ideal moment for the circulation of progressive news on Facebook. With print media hugely biased against Labour, the demand for fair representation of Labour's policies was met by social media. The *Independent* covered Labour's daily policy announcement straight, and saw its reporting shared widely online, with twelve of the twenty-five most-shared articles during the election coming from its stable. New outlets, sometimes dubbed the alt-left, such as the *Canary* and *Evolve Politics*, also witnessed dramatic increases in traffic. *Evolve Politics* says its monthly traffic grew from 150,000 hits per month to 1.4 million. Another left-wing site, *Another Angry Voice*, produced the top two most-shared articles of the election.[22]

This opening was short-lived. After Trump's election in 2016 and the Cambridge Analytica controversy, Facebook changed its algorithm to downgrade politics from users' timelines. Since then, the algorithm has changed without transparency, each time seeming to downgrade progressive news sources, while Twitter admits giving right-wing content 'more algorithmic amplification'.[23] Progressive forces cannot rely on platforms whose owners can be influenced by our opponents and by aims that are at odds with ours. If we look to the Global South, we can see how Facebook is weaponised against the left. In Bolivia's 2019 election, bots and fake accounts spread lies and spurious attacks about the government of Evo Morales and the Movement for Socialism. That election ended in a US-backed, anti-indigenous, hard-right coup, egged on by false pronouncements on social media and by the Organization of American States. Sophie Zhang, the Facebook official responsible for overseeing this public space who turned whistleblower, said she had 'blood on [her] hands'.[24]

Yet the media's ability to shape public perceptions rests on less-firm ground than it might first appear. It is extremely effective at leading opinion regarding the subjects of huge, concerted campaigns. This active distortion is why, according to a 2013 Ipsos Mori poll, the public believed that 15 per cent of girls under sixteen got pregnant, that a quarter of the benefit bill was lost to fraud, that the UK spent more on foreign aid than pensions or education, that 24 per cent of the population were Muslim and that nearly a third of the population were migrants.[25] Every one of these issues had been the focus of concerted campaigns of fearmongering by substantial sections of the media. A similar dynamic could be seen in Corbyn's personal ratings, which sank under sustained media attack until he could speak in his own voice with less mediation, such as in the 2017 general election, aided by rules on broadcaster election impartiality. Likewise, the manner of the reporting of antisemitism in the Labour Party during Corbyn's tenure distorted public perceptions. A 2019 Survation poll found that the public thought a third of Labour members – close to 200,000 people – had faced accusations of antisemitism, rather than the reality of less than 0.3 per cent.[26]

These statistics might make for gloomy reading, but in reality the media has comprehensively failed to construct a total right-wing public common sense. In fact, on a range of issues, there's a basic social-democratic common sense, which in some cases is to the left of anything that Labour argued for under Corbyn. Two-thirds of the public support a £15 minimum wage, which would represent a rise of over 50 per cent on current rates. Large majorities consistently say that the rich are paying too little in tax, and support taxing wealth at the same or higher rates than income from work.[27]

Concrete policy demands – the Green New Deal, a national care service, a wealth tax, public ownership, rent controls, a higher minimum wage and so on – are both popular and relatively well understood. Over two-thirds of the British public do not trust the banks, and almost three-quarters feel they should have faced stiffer penalties after the financial crisis. Even companies that are much more popular than banks face public concern. A 2020 Survation poll found 69 per cent of the public thought that Amazon was too powerful.[28] This social-democratic common sense is found in new industries too, with majorities in favour of regulating the gig economy by changing employment law to end bogus self-employment, and by requiring platforms to negotiate with a trade union and have worker representatives on their boards. Most of those under forty-five who were canvassed thought that gig-economy platforms should be taken into public ownership if they repeatedly fail to offer their workers fair pay and conditions.[29] Corbyn's response to the Manchester Arena terrorist bombings in 2017, when he called for an end to the War on Terror and presented the link between 'wars our government has supported or fought in other countries and terrorism here at home', provoked outrage across the political-media class. But a YouGov poll conducted in the immediate aftermath found that 53 per cent of the public believe that 'wars the UK has supported or fought are responsible, at least in part, for terror attacks against the UK'; only 24 per cent disagreed.[30]

Of course, large sections of the media could run concerted campaigns to reduce the progressive majority on policy issues. Their task will be made easier by the absence of traffic coming the other way from Labour's current front bench.[31] But such campaigns will struggle against a very high base rate and a startling lack of credibility. Trust in the media is low. The British printed press is the least trusted in Europe, and trust in TV news is below the European average.[32] It is not a foregone conclusion that this media will be able to police acceptable thought and prop up the political economic system on behalf of those who own it. Independent media, such as Novara, and successful digital channels, such as Momentum's, are still places where we can develop our arguments, clarify important lines on key issues and cover stories that other outlets do not.[33]

As Stuart Hall argued, when our opponents aim for a hegemonic political project, it is wise to learn from them – not because we wish to cave in to them, but in order to arrive at a realistic assessment of their strength.[34] The right has a media ecosystem to create outrage. Governments can do things such as fly patrol planes over the Channel to create a spectacle. Socialists lack the mass-media ecosystem and the bully pulpit to grab attention. But we have movements that can. What will be heard by people not paying close attention and what story do we want our controversies to tell them? What's our Churchill statue and our Channel patrol? Antagonism, direct action and controversy can make news, change opinions and set the political weather, whether they come from the left or the right.[35]

The openings created through movement populist spectacle will need to be taken up by progressives with large platforms and access to the media. The New Economy Organisers Network (NEON) already does important and underappreciated work in training and promoting progressive voices in broadcast studios.[36] It deserves support. But it is not enough on its own. The left bloc's secretariat can help tremendously with training, briefing and securing opportunities for Socialist Campaign Group MPs, trade unionists, intellectuals and social-movement activists, and then clipping their appearances for social media.

Each campaign can contribute to the next through developing the skills and experiences of activists. I saw this at first hand many times, but one particular example sticks in my memory: the Youth Climate Strike demonstration on Friday, 20 September 2019 in London, part of a global day of action for the climate involving an estimated 4 million people. There were 100,000 teenagers crammed into Millbank in Westminster. I was there with Jeremy Corbyn, who received a rapturous response when addressing the demonstration and thanking the participants for forcing the issue of climate change onto the political agenda. A double-decker bus was used as the speakers' platform, with the crowd spilling down Millbank on one side and organisers and press on the other. Here I saw a teenager with a clipboard, probably no older than sixteen, directing various broadcast cameras to capture and pool the best shots so all the broadcasters could use them. Ten years ago, few on the left had experience managing broadcasters to our advantage. Now there are several, including teenagers across the country activated by the Fridays for Future.

We can bring these stories the attention they deserve through movement-driven spectacle. We can force our opponents to discuss what they would rather not. The more time spent on our terrain is less time on theirs. Big polluters, City investors, dodgy landlords, rip-off bosses, tax cheats and media barons beware.

Socialist education

It has become fashionable on the left after Labour's defeat to highlight the pressing need for political education. We must be careful to not see defeat as an excuse to hole up in the seminar room, where too much of the left has been stranded since the defeats of the organised working class in the 1980s. Political education is primarily political exposure that encourages the development of confidence to act for yourself and collectively. Theory, history and analysis should all be in service of that advance, which is emotional and collective as much as it is intellectual and individual. The greatest teacher is the viscera of action.

The left bloc, through The World Transformed and others, could adopt political education in this more activist form. Each struggle throughout the bloc is an opportunity to advance political education. A campaign for jobs and decarbonisation at British Gas, for example, could help teach about privatisation – and how we can act against it – in a way that a reading group just could not. Or a campaign for public ownership of water could teach people about neoliberalism, through reading, videos and shareholder stunts at the AGMs of privatised utilities.

Movement self-education must ensure state power is taken seriously as a site of struggle.[37] Political education efforts – such as The World Transformed, the Political Education Project and trade union political-education programmes – should develop a course in state theory and practice. Such a course should be made available to shop stewards, community organisers, socialist MPs and their staff, councillors and future candidates, as well as grassroots activists. In addition to providing a detailed assessment of the contemporary British state's workings, it would combine the work of theorists such as Ralph Miliband, Nicos Poulantzas, André Gorz and Leo Panitch with the practical experiences of leftists operating within the state, either historically in the UK or abroad.

We must also finally learn how to talk about Labour antisemitism or left antisemitism, because neither actually existing antisemitism nor the bogus allegations is going away any time soon. To deny the existence of antisemitism on the left, or to capitulate to the false media narrative about its valence and extent, would both condemn us to immobilised marginality. Instead, we must have the capacity for self-criticism and self-confidence.

The antisemitism controversy under Corbyn's leadership had three interrelated elements. The first was that while only a tiny minority of Labour members are antisemites – as we have noted, there were cases against around 0.3 per cent of members under Corbyn's leadership – ignorance about antisemitism is more pervasive.[38] Cases were dealt with too slowly, ignorance wasn't sufficiently addressed and empathy was too often lacking. The second element was how anti-socialists, both within the Labour Party and without, over-stated antisemitism's scale and virulence dramatically, in a heavily mediatised moral panic that also scared Jewish people. The perception of Labour antisemitism towers over the actuality like King Kong over a gorilla; the gorilla must be tackled, but doing so will be harder if we are scanning the skyline for its more terrifying giant cousin. The third element was how antisemitism is defined, and the role this definition plays within discussions of Israel and Palestine. Some argue that anti-Zionism is 'the new antisemitism', a notion that prominent scholars and anti- and non-Zionist Jews, as well as some Zionist Jews, vigorously reject.[39] Following this logic would render much activism by or in support of Palestinians antisemitic by definition; indeed, this attitude led Labour Friends of Israel chair Joan Ryan to describe Palestinian flags at Labour conference as 'a weapon against Jewish people'.[40] This disagreement was at the root of the row over the application of the International Holocaust Remembrance Alliance definition of antisemitism, whose accompanying examples mainly relate to Israel. We have already seen efforts to render *ipso facto* antisemitic any support for the right of return of dispossessed Palestinians, discussion of the Nakba or the labelling of Israel an apartheid state. They are not.

Municipal lessons

Since education is more than studying, socialists should seek practical experience in using the state for progressive ends through local and devolved government. Councils have a bad reputation. Some are corrupt, others ineffective. Their powers have been stripped down with the aim of reducing them to little more than bodies responsible for the implementation of austerity. While there are many brilliant Labour councillors, others view the job as a stepping stone to something better or a reward for knocking on doors and stuffing envelopes. But local government can provide an opportunity for socialists not only to experience public administration and to operate within the state, but also to stimulate movements and do some good for their communities. It will strengthen our capacity to take the reins of central government when the next surge comes.

Despite the increased representation of socialists in local government over the past few years, mainly through a natural churn in selections, no coherent programme for municipal socialism was developed under Corbyn. There are too few success stories, and those that exist, such as Preston or Salford, are too little known. Yet developing examples of municipal socialism is a vital part of a socialist strategy. The concentration of Labour's membership, including its left membership, in metropolitan areas is often viewed as a weakness, especially following the loss of so many seats in small and medium-sized towns in the 2019 general election. Efforts to strengthen the membership and its socialist orientation in the so-called red wall – such as the No Holding Back initiative of Jon Trickett, Ian Lavery and Laura Smith – deserve support. But the density of an urban activist base also provides opportunities. Corbynism was by no means just a phenomenon in cities, but it did have the greatest purchase among the emerging 'new working class' of renters, precarious workers and the over-indebted that is concentrated in them. There is a substantial constituency of support for which municipal socialism could cater.

At least a portion of this opportunity for socialists could be realised through the Labour Party, which still has relatively democratic rules around the selection of council candidates. In the face of bureaucratic stitch-ups from Labour's regional offices, socialists should make a concerted effort, with the support of Momentum and left-led trade unions, to replace anti-socialist, status quo Labour councillors with socialist, movement-connected ones. These changes have already been taking place organically, with Momentum developing a socialist councillors' network and explicitly focusing on building municipal socialism, but a more public and active effort could win left majorities on the Local Campaign Forums that vet candidates and manage the procedures for local selections.

To do so effectively, the active minority on the local Labour left must do more to encourage the inactive majority. A public plan to build a programme for municipal socialism around the country, winning positive change for people and providing socialists with hands-on government experience, could help to galvanise the support needed from the more passive members. The left bloc could bring national attention to a campaign to win changes in town halls across the country, but a popular policy programme must be developed, alongside training for would-be councillors, to ensure it could be delivered.

More socialist-led councils could provide a boost to our movements. The Greater London Council, for example, stimulated and supported movements in the capital in the 1980s by opening up County Hall and giving grants to local groups. Progressive bulwarks in local government could aid today's movements in a similar way. By bringing services back in-house, councils could establish a floor under pay and conditions, and create decent, unionised jobs in their area. Councils could further support union drives in major local employers, using council communications to champion trade unions and only commissioning services from unionised companies. Socialist councils could inject new life into decaying high streets and sad parades by turning over empty shops to a variety of social uses. Spaces could be created for community organisations, support groups, social centres, labour, tenants' and unemployed movement organising; or they could be used as incubators for new co-ops, social enterprises, mutual aid groups and public interest companies. In this way, socialist councils could help to deepen the progressive organising and community support already taking place in their areas.

Such a strategy would not only support movements but also begin to lay the basis of a programme for a socialist-led national government, just as the London County Council did for the Attlee administration. In *Red Metropolis*, Owen Hatherley outlines the successes of the LCC in the 1930s in providing free healthcare, public transport and housing as well as administering public utilities.[41] While freedom for action is restricted by Tory legislation and limited funding, today's municipal socialism could demonstrate on a local level what is achievable nationally – participatory budgeting, mass council housing, publicly owned buses, Community Wealth Building, even a Green New Deal. As well as providing an opportunity to improve the lives of some people in a given neighbourhood, building left strength in local government will give some cadres experience in grappling with state machinery. In the process, we can learn from cutting-edge examples of progressive municipal government, such as Barcelona's public management of data, and develop global networks of municipal socialists.

Internationalist struggle

While we mine local and devolved government for experience to ready our advance at the national level, we can't believe that we can build socialism in one country. Capitalism is a global system, its value chains stretching from the mines of Chile to the factories of China to the financial laundering of the City and the supermarket shelves near you.[42] To build an alternative that confronts the crises we face, we must also expand our horizons internationally.

Authoritarian nationalists – Donald Trump, Jair Bolsonaro, Narendra Modi and to a lesser degree Boris Johnson – aided Covid-19's spread, but it is the global system's normal functioning that has turbocharged and extended it into further devastating waves. This rampantly unequal system prevents public health from being placed ahead of private profit or beggar-thy-neighbour nationalism. It has made health systems, particularly those of many poorer states, extremely vulnerable to the novel coronavirus: even before the pandemic struck, sixty-four lower-income countries were forced to pay more to lenders than towards their own citizens' health.[43] Round after round of IMF-mandated austerity has further undermined public health systems. In 2019, Ecuador dismissed 3,680 of its public sector health workers as part of the government's agreement with the IMF. During the pandemic, the country has had the world's second-highest number of excess deaths. Academics project that almost half of the world's countries will face austerity in 2022 and 2023 in response to the pandemic.[44]

Billionaires, meanwhile, have stuffed their offshore bank accounts during the pandemic. Oxfam has calculated that their wealth increased by an unfathomable $3.9 trillion in

2020, thanks in large part to coordinated central bank actions at the beginning of the pandemic to inflate asset prices.[45] No such concerted action has benefited the Global South: by the end of 2020, less than 1 per cent of global pandemic recovery funds had gone there, despite being home to the majority of the earth's population.[46] This financing gap, calculated at $2.5 trillion, could have been partially closed by the IMF through Special Drawing Rights, an international reserve asset created by the fund. But this is not what the global financial system and its managing institutions are set up to do.

This unequal system has shaped the pandemic. The British government is opposed to lifting intellectual property rules to make possible a speedy global vaccine roll-out. The European Parliament voted to waive intellectual property restrictions on vaccines, only to see the European Commission enforce them at the WTO. Without these restrictions, enough vaccines for the whole world could have been produced in one year.[47] If the Global North heeded the concrete proposals from South Africa and India to allow Global South countries to produce generic versions of vaccines without penalties, the pandemic would end sooner and lives and livelihoods would be saved.

Starmer's Labour has abandoned internationalist solutions and instead tucks in behind the government on all major international questions. Russia's brutal war on Ukraine, the revived possibility of nuclear-armed warfare between Russia and the United States, and the renewed confidence of establishment supporters of liberal empire make the development of a peace and anti-nuclear movement all the more pressing. It is incumbent on socialists to develop and articulate a clear internationalist, anti-imperialist politics in an era of the breakdown of US hegemony, which will no doubt produce monsters.

This internationalist lens must be applied to all our core demands and campaigns. If the Green New Deal is our recovery plan, it should be global. To make the Green New Deal more than an effective public works programme in the UK, we will need to develop policies and campaigns to free the whole world from the shackles of debt and austerity, to enable everyone to share in the technology developed in the Global North, and to end the offshoring of Britain's emissions.

British leftists should also support and learn from a resurgent Latin American left. If not a full Pink Tide, the region is at least experiencing a shift back towards the left: Andrés Manuel López Obrador has been elected in Mexico; the left Peronists have returned in Argentina; there has been an astounding democratic defeat of the coup regime in Bolivia; socialist schoolteacher Pedro Castillo was elected president of Peru; Xiomara Castro, Honduras's first female president and a self-described democratic socialist, has found triumph; Venezuela has continued to resist US regime-change efforts; Chile is drafting a new constitution and elected young leftist Gabriel Boric president; Gustavo Petro – dominant in the polls at the time of this writing – is leading a progressive coalition aimed at fully implementing peace in Colombia after a half century of bloodshed, and it looks likely that Luiz Inázio Lula da Silva will return as president of Brazil. These states will face attack throughout the next decade from international financial institutions, the US empire, corporate power and Western media. In Ecuador, Facebook has restricted the activities of former president Rafael Correa and his supporters with little accountability. Nor should we view these attacks as something happening *over there*. Just days after a number of Trump's accounts were deleted by social media platforms, an Instagram post critical of the Johnson government's pandemic response, by Labour MP Zarah Sultana, was blocked by moderators.

Neither injustice nor inspiration stops at our borders: victory or a defeat in one place makes the same more likely in another. Our enemies are globally networked; so must we be. Companies learn from each other how to defeat national labour movements industrially and politically. Trade unionists already collaborate through global federations, but much more can be done to build active solidarity between workers and struggles across multinational supply chains, which should be the horizon for organising. Thickening progressive internationalist networks should be a supplementary aim of any campaign with a global dimension. British socialists have a duty to be internationalist, as our country has and continues to play an outsized role in the construction and maintenance of a grotesquely unjust global order that inflicts hardship on billions to inflate the offshore bank accounts of the few. An internationalist turn for the British left would also strengthen us in three ways. First, it will equip us with an alternative to the authoritarian nationalism championed by Priti Patel. Second, it will inject knowledge and momentum from other struggles into our own. Third, it will advance the global struggles within which our national efforts sit.

But for a socialist internationalism to be effective, it must be rooted in majoritarianism at home. The single most effective thing we can do for global justice is to win in the UK – and win we can.

5

Party and State

In *For a Left Populism*, Chantal Mouffe argues that although recent protest movements 'have played a role in the transformation of political consciousness, it is only when they have been followed by structured political movements, ready to engage with political institutions, that significant results have been achieved'. There is a sequence of events that leads from the Indignados to Podemos, Occupy to Sanders.[1] As a result of our defeat in 2019, the British left has slipped down the snake and must start back up the ladder. The existence of strong, well-organised and interconnected movements will be the foundation for building a left-wing electoral front with a real chance of winning elections and entering the state.

We must take time to work out what that successful movement-party needs to look like. Whether that vehicle ends up having a Labour rose as its symbol or not, this essential work begins now.

Our process of exploration will inevitably include a testing of the limits of what can still be achieved through the post-Corbyn Labour Party. The left bloc's strategy requires a changed view towards Labour on the part of its progressive grassroots members. Rather than viewing the party as an expression of our politics and our identity – and therefore suffering real pain at each leadership failure or outrage – we should view it pragmatically as an institution through which we might be able to advance some of our politics and causes. Labour is an institution with some members and trade unions in the camp of progressive social forces and a parliamentary wing embedded within the state. This contradictory biloca-tion generates the desire to challenge the power structures of capitalist society, as well as the impulse to prop them up. The party is a site of struggle, a collective institution that we want to be able to use, in the same way we want to use other collective institutions. When the party is viewed in this way, membership of it doesn't sum up who you are politically, nor put you in the position of merely being a cheerleader for whoever happens to be in the shadow cabinet at the time.[2]

A party consists of its culture and practices, its policies and its personnel. To transform Labour, the balance of forces would need to be shifted on all three levels, and each level prised open to movement needs. The Corbyn years didn't get very far with this work. In the main, the party organised and held meetings largely as it always had. The content of what was discussed in local parties shifted to the left, but few constituency Labour parties became meaning-ful hubs of community or movement activism. Today, the party's internal democracy has been denuded by Starmer and David Evans. There are still opportunities for move-ment demands to gain attention though, and each leadership refusal to accept progressive policy motions at least educates the wider membership. A left bloc could exert indirect influence on the party through local-level campaigns that bring together movements, Momentum and others. This activity won't take place through the Labour Party, which these days seems irrelevant to many activists, but its proximity – lots of Labour members taking part, without their Labour hats on – will influence constituency parties. If members are engaging in meaningful political activity elsewhere, it should be psychologically easier to hold on to their party cards pragmatically. Their direct engagement with Labour could be limited to voting in internal elections and campaigning for good candidates.

On personnel, the Labour right will do everything it can to exclude the left from every position possible. The left bloc could help the different sections of our movement work together, as well as identify and promote powerful movement voices and community champions. The combined weight of all these forces would consolidate its position in internal party elections, especially if the left bloc were to be able to replace the fractious and undemocratic backroom bargaining model of the Centre-Left Grassroots Alliance for determining candidates for internal party elections and replace it with a democratic system.

These efforts to shift the balance of forces in the party and provide a greater movement focus would be a lifeline for the left's increasingly embattled MPs. Even the most movement-focused person with strong extra-parliamentary connections can fall victim to parliamentary cretinism if they spend too long in the Palace of Westminster. Bringing the Socialist Campaign Group MPs into the left bloc will help ward off this affliction. Most of all, our MPs should take confidence from being part of something much larger than themselves. The Parliamentary Labour Party is a lonely and hostile place for socialist MPs, with the party leadership readying to remove them. Knowing they are the parliamentary wing of a much larger, federated movement of movements would help give confidence to elected representatives that they can take clear lines independent of the leadership when necessary. With the leadership attacking both peace and environmental extra-parliamentary campaigners, movement-minded MPs will need a solid foundation from which to speak up.

A front-footed move that unites left forces in Labour with those not necessarily in the party, such as XR, BLM, Sisters Uncut, tenants' unions, DPAC, Stop the War and so on, would lead to conflict with the Starmer leadership. That conflict is already taking place, only most of the traffic is one way. As the struggle for the party intensifies, a new clarity of purpose should emerge. Either the left will slow down the great moving-right show through exerting real pressure the other way, keeping Labour open for the left; or Starmer's Blairite handlers will try to force a split. In the latter situation, the result would not be an organised pro–status quo Labour Party on the one hand and disorganised pro-change leftists on the other. Rather, we would see an organised pro–status quo Labour Party and an *organised* pro-change force with real social weight: seven to ten trade unions, Britain's biggest social movements, perhaps two dozen MPs, a few MSPs and MSs, perhaps hundreds of councillors and a pool of at least 300,000 former Labour members. All these elements could unite to form a new party that could conceivably gain the social and electoral weight, perhaps in alliance with the Greens or others, to surpass Labour as the main anti-Tory vehicle in one or two electoral cycles. Rather than worrying about Starmer and his enforcers' response, we should focus on getting organised.

A new model party

There is a two-fold fundamental challenge facing social-democratic parties in the industrial world. The first is how to graduate from being the junior partner within a neo-liberal system that has lost the consent of the majority. The second is how to hold together a constituency that contains a growing gulf. This means finding commonalities between those elements of the working class that benefited from Thatcherite and New Labour expansion in asset ownership and asset-price inflation, and a less well-represented, generally younger, more urban, more diverse, more precarious, more formally educated and less asset-rich working class. Together they make up the overwhelming majority of the population. This mission should inform our view on what kind of party can win, and win big, in this decade and the next.

We need fresh and original thinking. Before Corbyn's leadership, few on the left had seriously thought about what a democratic-socialist movement-party would look like in the twenty-first century.[3] What was the point? There seemed almost zero chance of building one. This absence hamstrung Momentum's early days as different political cultures jostled to create an organisational structure fit for the task ahead. I and others argued for representation for social movements on Momentum's national committee so that the organisation could act as a hinge between Labour under Corbyn and the diverse movements needed to transform society. This structure was not to be. But these principles should be actively considered for the governance of a transformational party, whatever it is called. Movement representatives on a national executive will help reduce parliamentary dominance. The left bloc's structure, however it works out, could begin to test out models and methods that break us out of our twentieth-century party mould.

We will also have to experiment with different models to nurture the greatest level of sustainable activity from the rank and file throughout the movement. Such models might include identifying activists in a given location who state a willingness to organise around a particular issue, and connecting them, for example via WhatsApp. Another strategy would be to develop campaigns in highly active, high-density areas, and then deploy resources to roll out these campaigns in less active areas.

We can develop new ways of running local or issue groups. The trade union branch model works for some types of activism, but certainly not all. A new model party's focus needs to shift away from internal elections to specific local positions and towards encouraging members to participate actively. The birth of Momentum could have offered alternative models but it quickly adopted the traditional labour-movement method – electing a chair, a secretary and so on – which generally benefited the most organised section of the left in each area, rather than maximising activity across the group as a whole. Democracy is about more than voting. It also requires participation.

That broader conception of democracy should be applied to policy and strategy development too. Labour's policy process was barely reformed while Corbyn was leader. The National Policy Forum, a Blair-era ruse to keep policy-making hidden behind closed doors and free from democratic control, was left intact. The number of motions members and trade unionists could debate at party conferences was expanded, but without much thought given to how these would be integrated into a workable party platform.

The 2019 party conference in Brighton was exciting because, for the first time, the base of the party was more advanced than the leadership. The conference floor voted for policies beyond the leadership, including a Green New Deal 2030, abolishing private schools and introducing a national care service. Most of the leadership team were less than delighted. These policies could cause headaches. Some motions were poorly drafted and now had to be managed. For example, the motion against private schools from the Abolish Eton campaign contained mutually contradictory policies.[4] The campaign, run by schoolteacher Holly Rigby, was superb and was rightly supported by the conference, but it shone a light on what little thought had been given to the role of members in setting strategy and detailed policy development.

The role of conference for a new model party should be to set the big strategic direction; it should not provide the detailed specifications of policy. Strategic questions are the ones that require full debate and decisions taken by the movement as a whole – few can be meaningfully considered at any one time. This need could be discharged by setting a limited quota for the number of strategic decisions to be taken at conference each year. These would set the direction. Conference could then mandate a committee to develop the detailed policy, which should include relevant trade unions, social movements and members with knowledge about the sector, alongside staff, technical advisors and thinkers. The relevant politicians should then have to report back to the following year's conference about how far they've developed the policy: popular support, the movement behind it, the technical implementation details, the outline of how it will work with government machinery, funding, and so on. That report could be accepted or rejected by conference. This process would give the movement as a whole the power to make big decisions on the top-line policies, and then provide scrutiny over whether they are on track.

'In and against the state'

We will never achieve fundamental social change if we ignore the question of state power. The state is not a neutral institution, but nor is it just the executive committee of the ruling class.[5] It is a force that shapes so many areas of our lives through laws and taxes, punishments and rewards. Not only must the left bloc advance a political plan for seizing the reins of the state, but we must also develop a strategy for transforming it. This is a messy business. It entails both involving ourselves with party politics and situating ourselves within state institutions, which are often set up against the interests of the many.

Some of the Corbyn team's struggles against Labour's bureaucracy and constant establishment assaults could be instructive as we turn our eyes towards the state. The tacit knowledge gained about handling obstructive elements of the party machine, how to handle the media and how to build institutional counter-power needs to be passed on to the wider movement. This knowledge must be coupled with an understanding of public policy, not as a technocratic exercise undertaken by a neutral state but ultimately as a means to transform the state, which is itself a complex site of class struggle.

Several leading lights of Corbynism followed directly in the footsteps of the 'in and against the state' approach advocated by people such as Tony Benn, Ralph Miliband and Leo Panitch. 'In and Against the State' was a 1979 pamphlet published in the immediate aftermath of Thatcher's election victory, by a working group of the Conference of Socialist Economists exploring how socialist 'state workers' could bring 'the struggle for socialism into . . . daily work'. Understandably, the phrase has since been used in Gramscian terms, proposing a war of position through existing state institutions.[6] But it also has a related set of meanings connected to a strategy which sees the state as a hostile, contested space that socialists should both seek to enter and develop the 'agental capacity for state transformation', as Leo Panitch and Sam Gindin put it.[7] John McDonnell frequently referred to this strategy while shadow chancellor. Speaking alongside Panitch at a 2018 *Red Pepper* event in London, McDonnell summarised the strategy as aiming to 'open the doors of that institution and transform the relationship from one of dominance into one of democratic engagement and participation'.

Notwithstanding this interesting line of thought, the Corbyn party's preparations for government were flawed. Plans for legislation were drawn up with the shadow teams but tended to treat the party programme as something that could be implemented through existing state machinery, without mass mobilisations and with little establishment backlash. After meetings with senior civil servants about Labour's 2019 policy programme, one senior member of Corbyn's team remarked that the civil service was 'genuinely excited' about enacting Labour's planned legislation. Such hopes would have melted on contact with reality.

If we wish to realise our long-term aspiration of winning office to transform state power, we cannot allow this short-coming to persist. Some may feel that such a focus on the state after Corbyn is quixotic given our distance from power. But we must use this time to develop our capacities to act in and against the state so that we are ready for the next surge. This state-focused orientation is not a parliamentary one – far from it. We must move beyond the parliamentary Leninism that implicitly governed much of the Corbyn project's strategic direction. Parliament is not where our movements are strongest, most dynamic, or most advanced.

To succeed in enacting far-reaching reforms, we must achieve a high level of organisation among progressive forces; a higher level of proficiency in navigating and resisting the many obstacles placed in their way; and an ability to mobilise mass support for our policies. An 'in and against the state' strategy requires all three elements to work in tandem, to achieve a radical shift in the balance of power, income and wealth. A basic and necessary step is winning elections within the current system, with the aim of making major changes that noticeably improve the lives of the over-whelming majority. But with power, we will have to go further, building people's self-confidence and capacities for collective self-government by making more fundamental changes to democratise the state, the economy and society.

A radical government must pass three categories of measures in the first term of office – and get the balance right. The first is a swathe of immediate, ameliorative measures, mainly using the state's existing policy levers, such as tax and spend, to improve lives both swiftly and noticeably. The second category comprises strong reforms, measures that will alter the social contract. They must be radical and attract opposition – not like Brown's tax credits, which have been undone, but like the minimum wage, which cannot be taken away because it was won through a high-profile struggle. The third consists of non-reformist reforms – those which push at the boundaries of the possible. Examples include the creation of the NHS in the 1940s and a universal basic dividend today. Achieving reforms of the third kind will depend more on the balance of forces in society and within the movement itself than on capacity of the state and its civil servants. If implemented effectively to overcome elite opposition, this package could have a ratchet effect, creating a dynamic momentum in a progressive direction. Every action must be situated in an understanding of where we are now and where we want to be. The essence for all reforms is to be radical and reflect common sense, while at the same time pushing the state in a democratic and socialist direction.

Take the first level, immediate ameliorative measures: it will be necessary to foreground policies such as raising the minimum wage, ending the public sector pay cap, providing immediate funding for schools, hospitals, social care and childcare, ending tuition fees, and so on, as well as how the wealthy and big business will pay for them. These are the reforms from which big groups of the electorate will immediately benefit. That first element can be relatively top-down and mediatised, and can be conducted, more or less, within the parameters of Westminster politics – while bringing about a substantial tilt to the left.

Then there is the second category of strong reforms – those that will face intense opposition and, for that reason, are not easily undone once in place. As already suggested, two New Labour policies are cases in point: the 1998 introduction of the minimum wage and tax credits. The latter policy resulted in more redistribution of income than the former, but proceeded by stealth. The succeeding Conservative government could dramatically reduce tax credits within a year of coming to power, whereas the minimum wage – a strong reform foisted on New Labour by trade union affiliates, though set at a low level – has been extended. Such reforms can shift the country's social settlement lastingly in a progressive direction. As such, they face serious opposition. To see these reforms through, a progressive government will need at least one organised section of society fighting for this key demand. These reforms bring social conflict to the fore and so can't just be announced as a good idea.

Consider the experience of the universal free broadband policy in the 2019 Labour election platform. It's a strong reform that would expand the social settlement in a progressive direction. It would provide a service that would then be held on to and fought for. But in 2019, that policy was in no way a popular demand. It stretched credibility because it had not come up from any organised force in society. Ahead of being in government, the party needs to work out which reforms will most advance the socialist project, and how it could stimulate demand for them. It must then set about doing so.

The third category, non-reformist reforms of the kind called for by André Gorz fifty-five years ago, has the potential for maximum social conflict and therefore requires the largest stimulation of social forces in support of them beforehand.[8] Rather than just advancing the social settlement, such reforms contain a dynamic within them to carry on shifting the balance of forces in the progressive direction. Imagine, for example, a policy to create a people's investment fund to bring stakes in strategic companies and sectors into public ownership and take significant stakes in infrastructure and investment projects. If that fund paid out a universal basic dividend to everyone in the country, there would emerge a mass constituency with a short-term as well as long-term material interest in democratising the economy. But for that to be delivered, it would have to overcome heavy resistance from capital and its political allies. That's why non-reformist reforms require extremely high levels of understanding and organisation to be successfully introduced.

This approach to reforms is an advance on where the Corbyn project left off. From 2017 onwards, both the party's machinery and the movement around the party, including think tanks and campaign groups, developed policies in too utopian a manner. Around the party, activists developed and won the party over to radical policies but with too little idea of sequencing, prioritisation and electoral appeal. Many within the party machinery – members of the shadow cabinet, their staff, people in the Corbyn and McDonnell offices, the staff in party headquarters – had an overly left-technocratic approach. Detailed policies were often developed as if they would be implemented by a neutral state machinery. The thinking behind the 2019 manifesto is nevertheless highly valuable and impressive, including the substantial documents that stand behind individual policies. Take the policy on pharmaceuticals: it consists of two sentences in the manifesto, with a detailed fifty-page report sitting behind it.[9] But that work needs to be combined with a more comprehensive idea of how these policies are going to become reality beyond draft legislation.

Here the movements that politically cohere with the new model party come to the fore. By developing and federating our movements through our bloc, we increase the chances of constructing a new model party with the will and skill to enter the state and thoroughly democratise it. Without such focused ambition, the onrushing climate collapse and violent inequality are likely to accelerate into sheer dystopia.[10]

6

Ways of Winning

A long-term strategy should be flexible enough to respond to contingent openings. It is for this reason that I resist both those who say that Labour is the only possible political vehicle for democratic socialist advance and equally those who say that Labour could never be such a vehicle. But a strategy also needs a theory of *intentional* social change.[1] While we can't know the future, we can sketch out what winning might look like, based on the plan laid out in this book.

To do so, I employ Erik Olin Wright's schema of 'logics of transformation': interstitial, evolutionary and ruptural. Interstitial change, commonly associated with anarchism, seeks to build the new within the shell of the old, as cracks open up in the ruling system. Evolutionary change, commonly associated with social democracy, seeks to build up power within the existing system so as to tilt it in a progressive direction. Ruptural change, commonly associated with revolutionary socialism, seeks to effect a dramatic shift from one system to another. 'All contain dilemmas, risks, and limits, and none of them guarantee success,' Olin

Wright comments. 'In different times and places, one or another of these modes of transformation may be the most effective, but often all of them are relevant.'[2]

Combining these logics of transformation in varying proportions, I offer four scenarios for a successful left bloc in the 2020s. What unites these 'four futures' is that they all involve progressive forces coming together in novel and powerful formations to build our power and reach towards a social majority.[3]

First future

The 2020s was a strange decade in British politics. It ended, much as it had begun, with a Tory in Downing Street. An interlude when there was a minority Labour government brought no substantial reforms, and turnout fell at successive general elections.

But as audiences for Westminster's stultifying stage show dwindled, more of the population was actively engaged in campaigns on a variety of issues. The Conservative Party tended to win elections, but the country, if polls are to be believed, moved in a left and socially progressive direction, although social polarisation remained high. These attitudes rarely received formal political expression, but when a campaign, often championed by a celebrity, cut through into the media, government policy changed swiftly.

Politicians of all parties often felt they were on the back foot, trapped between the rising demands of the population, the realities of the climate transition and their establishment power bases. Both the blue and red Westminster teams were able to pass some laws in the teeth of organised popular opposition, but they also faced major defeats and embarrassing U-turns. Authoritarian legislation designed to further restrict most forms of activism, protest and trade unionism were defeated by an unusual alliance of street mobilisations, strikes, sit-ins and the still unreformed House of Lords.

As the decade unfolded, organising across progressive movements became more advanced, coherent and confident. With only limited, although significant, allies in Parliament, movements took it upon themselves to win substantial policy goals from below. This approach improved work for the majority in the UK, as the labour movement made its weight felt. Nearly half of all workers, whether among the country's 8.5 million union members or not, were now covered by collective bargaining agreements. Almost all major sectors of the economy had new effective minimum wages, agreements for gradually reducing working hours, and some even had a structure of consultation and pay increases to accompany technological advances. These significant changes were gained through a combination of piecemeal victories won by workers, forward-thinking union leaders and major national campaigns, including the general strike of 2026. Unions found support for their actions across society, despite media demonisation, as movements joined hands. The general strike, in particular, had a rainbow effect, bringing together a wide range of organisations and demands. It was only diffused by the Conservative prime minister calling a general election, which she lost.

With the global average temperature already 1.5 degrees above pre-industrial levels, signs of climate breakdown abound. No UK government took the lead on decarbonising the British economy, but rates of decarbonisation nevertheless increased through activist pressure. Some dirty, energy-intensive activities were made uneconomic through persistent disruption of sites or embarrassment of parent companies. For some major corporations, polluting in Britain became too much of a hassle. The decarb rate, as it is known, became as prominent as GDP and inflation, another figure that stalked the decade. Each government tried to improve it in the face of mass pressure from below, including monthly strikes on Fridays across the whole economy, not only by schoolchildren.

Footage of a violent hate crime and the death of a Muslim youth in police custody caused a public uproar. Protests led by Black Lives Matter and the Muslim Council of Britain, and supported by the forces of the left bloc, spread around the country. In one West Yorkshire town, local activists set up a community oversight board for local policing. Some council workers used council resources to support the oversight board and were sacked, prompting a walkout of council staff, led by their union. The strike claimed national attention, leading to community police oversight boards being set up around the country and demanding recognition from police forces. Backed up by a national campaign for greater police transparency and community consultation, some forces agreed to hand over information and consult with community groups. After initially denouncing the boards as 'interfering with crime-stopping', the home secretary hailed the move as 'a new era of policing by consent'. The boards were not put on a legislative footing.

Funding for prevention and prosecution of domestic violence doubled in the 2020s under sustained pressure from the feminist movement after a series of well-publicised cases. One of the general strike's demands, led by feminists in the labour movement, was for mandatory training about sexual violence and a transparent, independent complaints process for all companies with 250 staff or more. All parties, apart from the hard-right Future Britain Party, pledged to carry out this reform at the 2027 election, and it was written into law by the new Parliament.

Social care provision for the elderly improved marginally over the course of the decade, though a wealth tax was not forthcoming. Working-age disabled people were initially left out of an emergency government funding package. In response, DPAC and allies across the left bloc engaged in a series of eye-catching stunts, including rushing the stage at the MOBO Awards, where activists unveiled a banner reading 'Disabled Lives Matter. Care and support now.' Thirty-eight local councils were taken to court in a coordinated wave of legal action for failing to provide statutory care; twelve of these put up no defence, blaming central government cuts, and backed the activists' demands. The government agreed to a new funding settlement which saw social care and support for independent living for the disabled increase in real terms by 5 per cent a year for five years.

Record numbers of young people went to university and began their working lives under a mountain of debt. The student movement joined forces with many other organisations to build a coalition of those holding tuition debt. After five years of campaigning, trying a range of tactics, they secured a small write-down on student debt deemed unpayable. Younger people were also at the forefront of a new wave of tenants' organising. Rent strikes were organised against six of the UK's ten biggest landlords, leading to agreements for no rent rises for five years. No-fault evictions were finally banned too, almost ten years after Prime Minister Theresa May suggested they might be. But it took a private member's bill from a backbench MP to secure the legislative change.

While UK governments had to be forced to make progressive changes to the law, some local and devolved governments delivered proactive change. Both Wales and Scotland outstripped England in decarbonisation and led on social provision, but independence remained blocked off. More left-led Labour councils sprang up around the country, delivering a programme of council house building, participatory budgeting, in-sourcing of services, community wealth-building and local environment planning. By the end of the decade, these councils allied with the democratic socialist mayors of London, Greater Manchester, the West Midlands, West Yorkshire, South Yorkshire and North Tyneside to develop and coordinate a 'Green New Deal from below', arguing that the UK government had failed to deliver. Some began to experiment with liquid voting and direct democracy for some decisions.

These local and regional radical politics were at odds with the Labour leadership's turgid national approach. The so-called civil war in the party did not end, as neither left nor right could fully win out. More socialists were elected into Parliament in the decade, but Keir Starmer's successor was not from the left. Neither force yet had the power to bring the other firmly to heel.

The 2020s were a decade of building power in the gaps, with no opportunity to convert that power into office. Despite the urgency of enacting deeper and far-reaching change, this was nevertheless a form of winning for the left. It achieved a series of significant victories to improve the lives of the majority and prepare the way for much more major advances.

Second future

The 2020s was a turbulent decade in British politics. Both the Conservative and Labour Parties seemed to spend much of it in a civil war, and opinion poll leads seesawed between the two. Neither was held in high regard by the public. Turnout fell at each successive election.

But as the media's attention was focused on the Westminster tug of war, with no leader of either party managing to stay in the post long, more of the population, according to polls, was actively engaged in campaigns away from frontline politics. Polarisation was high, as first struggles over how to respond to Covid and then other culture war divides came and went. Underneath the radar, however, if polls are to be believed, the country moved in a left and socially progressive direction. These attitudes have only recently received formal political expression with the substantial change in the opposition Labour Party.

After a few years of defeat and retreat in the party, the Labour left looked down and out. The situation seemed even more dire when the race to succeed Sir Keir Starmer QC as leader was won narrowly by a young figure from the party's right pledging to turn Labour into the UK's Democrats, 'the second party of power, like in the USA'. Despite a rebrand, a shift to the right politically and proposed rule changes to limit both member and trade union influence in the party, Labour's new leadership was finally unable to drive out the left. This failure was mainly due to the significant levels of social protest and dramatic mobilisations through the period, which structured so much of the political debate of the time.

The party's leadership was wrongfooted by movement victories, which involved many rank-and-file Labour members. A strike wave for sectoral collective bargaining agreements seemed to offer the leadership an opportunity to break decisively with militancy and demonstrate its unshakeable support for the status quo. The only problem was that the workers kept winning. As shop-floor organising brought more and more of the economy under collective agreements, the leadership was forced to back off.

Each wave of protest from below was met with bipartisan opposition – one party full-throated, the other embarrassed – but activists often managed to win. Despite the Labour Party's outright opposition to movements combined with its cowardly silence on the problems of the day, it benefited politically from this unrest. In 2026, the wave of protests and campaigns came to a head with a general strike. The Conservative government was split over how to handle the breakdown in social peace. The winning faction, whose members the media termed Gaullists after former French president Charles de Gaulle, decided to defeat the strike at the ballot box and called a general election. Supporters of this strategy believed that it would be successful, just as the French conservatives did in the snap election following May '68. They argued that the Labour Party, also hopelessly divided and reactive in its approach to such a major national mobilisation, would not do well. In the end, turnout was low and voters punished the big two parties, with smaller parties registering protest votes, including one self-styled direct democracy 'pop up party' which won 10 per cent of the vote, but no seats. Labour became the largest party in Parliament and formed a minority government.

The election did end the general strike. A few of its demands, such as mandatory training about sexual violence and a transparent, independent complaints process for all companies with 250 or more staff, were met by the new government. But social peace did not return. The UK's movements continued their advances, with more coordinated actions and campaigns.

The Labour government sought to resist many of these campaigns in the name of order and representative parliamentary democracy. But the party's left flank effectively abandoned the government, championing demands from below. The government did not last long, losing a vote of no confidence after less than two years. It was punished at the subsequent election, which returned a Conservative majority government. During the Labour administration, it had become commonplace for commentators to refer to Labour as two parties: one in government, the other in opposition. After the crushing defeat, its leadership switched. The left was now in charge.

Unlike the previous time that the left had led the Labour Party, the new leadership engaged in explicit and rapid party transformation. Dubbed 'shock therapy' by the media and outraged MPs, the entire party apparatus was overhauled with a major fundraiser launched to pay for a wave of voluntary redundancies of Labour right staff. Next, the whole rulebook was rewritten. The new edition, endorsed by a special conference, turned Labour into a movement-party along the lines of a blueprint developed earlier in the decade. In response, a third of Labour MPs left the party, a move appreciated by the leadership, which said it looked forward to welcoming new MPs from the movements that were doing so much to change British society for the better.

Movements won more from Labour than just candidates for office. The party explicitly viewed itself as the political arm of movements, which it coordinated alongside championing their demands. These were brought together and given focus with Labour's signature policy of a Green New Deal for the many, not the few.

Some of Labour's policies were trialled in miniature in local and devolved government, which took a decided turn to the left and became a site of experimentation, including with new forms of democracy, such as participatory budgeting and liquid voting. Labour still ran many councils in the old way, with some right-wing councillors defecting to the ex-Labour MPs' new political vehicle. But Labour's left-wing local government leaders became a significant force in politics, issuing challenges to the Conservative government and stimulating campaigns and movements in their areas. The national leadership promoted their efforts.

The decade closed with Labour ahead in the polls and striking a confident pose. The party's ability to use spectacle and controversy as a way to highlight important issues helped to counteract the intense media hostility it faced. It had another weapon in its arsenal too: a million members linked to movements active in every community of the country. For the first time in perhaps one hundred years, the Labour Party didn't look, sound and feel like just a team of politicians in Westminster; rather, it was a living, breathing part of everyday life for millions of people wanting a better world.

Third future

The 2020s was a turbulent decade in British politics. Both the Conservative and Labour parties seemed to spend much of it in a civil war and opinion poll leads seesawed between the two. Neither was held in high regard by the public. Turnout fell at each successive election.

But as the media's attention was focused on the Westminster tug of war, with no leader of either party managing to stay in post long, more of the population, according to polls, was actively engaged in campaigns away from frontline politics. Polarisation was high, as first struggles over how to respond to Covid and then other culture war divides came and went. Underneath the radar, however, if polls are to be believed, the country moved in a left and socially progressive direction. These attitudes have only recently received formal expression in a major new political party.

After a few years of defeat and retreat in the Party, the Labour left looked down and out. The situation looked even direr when the race to succeed Sir Keir Starmer QC as leader was won narrowly by a young figure from the party's right pledging to turn Labour into the UK's Democrats, 'the second party of power, like in the USA'. Following a rebrand, a shift to the right politically and proposed rule changes to limit both member and trade union influence in the party, Labour's new leadership was ready to finally drive out the left. Its opportunity came amid a strike wave for sectoral collective bargaining agreements, supported by many rank-and-file Labour members.

First, the leadership opposed a strike of fast-food workers organised by the Bakers' union, as 'unrealistic dreams of the snob left that prefers falafel and cappuccino to Big Macs'. The Labour leader, who himself claimed to have worked in McDonald's as a teenager, labelled the union's members 'troublemakers who fortunately play no role in the Labour Party or the responsible trade union movement', and pledged a broader crackdown on activists. These comments spurred the left into open revolt.

The final split came over the nurses' strike. The Labour leadership labelled the strikes for better pay and safe staffing levels 'a danger to the public'. Anyone who attended its picket lines had 'blood on their hands and no place in the modern, democratic Labour Party'.

The Labour left defied the party leadership. The pickets were enormous. The public was with the nurses despite near blanket media coverage about deaths on hospital wards and irresponsible radicals stirring up trouble. Twenty-five Labour MPs, four Labour MSPs, eight council leaders, seven affiliated trade unions, four non-affiliated trade unions, the biggest three tenants' unions and several social movements announced they were forming a new party. Within a month the party had 300,000 members, more than double Labour's figure.

The new party formed on a blueprint laid out over the previous years and was an innovator in technology to support grassroots activism. Grassroots and movement support was needed to advance the party in the face of intense media onslaught. Taking comments from rank-and-file members out of context and presenting them as a national position of the party was a regular Fleet Street trick.

Rather than being embarrassed by the attacks, the new party approached them head-on. It argued that it was a mass people's movement, and sometimes ordinary people would say things that weren't correct or sophisticated. 'It just shows,' a prominent member said in an interview, 'that we really are the political arm of the movements of this country that represent the British people's yearning for a better life for themselves and their families and justice for all.'

The party explicitly viewed itself as the political arm of movements, with whom it coordinated and whose demands it championed. These were brought together and given focus with a signature policy of a Green New Deal for the many, not the few.

Nimble alliances had to be made, producing a patchwork across the country. The party formed partial electoral pacts with Welsh Labour, the Green Party of England and Wales and some Labour-led councils. The party pointed to examples of its policies trialled in miniature in local and devolved government, whether under a Labour left or its own banner. Not all of the left-led councils immediately joined the party, depending mainly on the phase of their electoral cycle, but several were sites of experimentation with new forms of democracy, including participatory budgeting and liquid voting.

The decade closed with a Conservative government in office, huge volatility in the polls and a cycle of major movement mobilisations forcing change on politics. This agenda from below was championed by the new party, which jostled with Labour to be the main home for anti-Tory votes. The historic struggle within Labour between those who wanted to challenge the system and those who wanted to prop it up would now take place in the electoral arena.

Fourth future

The 2020s saw the old die and the new finally born in British politics. The tumult excited much of the population and terrified others, whose fears were stoked by the UK's billionaire-owned media.

The spark seemed small enough: an increase in hospital car-parking charges in the name of reducing car use to tackle climate change. The policy came at a time of mounting public anger over official inaction in a context of soaring billionaire wealth, falling living standards and frequent extreme weather caused by global average temperatures already over 1.5 degrees centigrade above pre-industrial levels. Much of the media was dumbfounded by NHS staff, commuters and environmentalists mobilising under the banner of a 'Green New Deal for the many, not the few'.

From the car parks of the NHS estate, the protests spread like wildfire. More and more issues and movements clamoured to be involved. The protests combined the experimentation and surprise of horizontal organising with the focus of verticality through movement and left coordination. Each attempt to stop the protests seemed instead to metastasise them. Soon major bank buildings were occupied, Parliament was surrounded, hedge funds picketed, polluters blockaded and private health care offices rendered unusable. Something had to give.

The protestors produced their shortlist of five core demands under the Green New Deal rubric, including popular demands from all the major movements. Snap polling showed between 65 and 80 per cent support for each. The movements, united with left forces in Parliament, formed a small negotiating team that occupied Sky News's studio in

Westminster, where it demanded the government come and
negotiate live on TV. After three more days of steep share-
price declines and pressure on the pound, the government
sent its negotiating team. With five days of talks complete,
the leaders of the left bloc gave the government twenty-
four hours to produce its final offer. It was put to a national
vote via an online liquid voting platform that the alliance
of movements and left political forces had set up. The nego-
tiators recommended rejecting the government's offer,
claiming its paltry nature showed the entire political system
needed an overhaul. The government's terms were rejected,
and the occupations and strikes continued. The movement
now had a single demand: a new constitution to create a
fresh politics that would be responsive to popular needs
and wants.

Sensing an opportunity to kick the can and diffuse the
energy of the protests in the technicalities of a democratic
process, the government agreed to a referendum on whether
to have a new written constitution drafted by a newly elected
constituent assembly. The document that body produced
would be rejected or confirmed by a further referendum.

The first referendum overwhelmingly demanded a new
constitution. Elections to the constituent assembly were
humiliating for the established parties. They huddled
together as a shrunken third force between the majority
Alliance of the Many, which represented a range of movements and campaign groups from every region and nation
of the country with candidates decided on through the
liquid voting democracy platform, and Order and Stability,
a new force opposed to the entire process.

In eighteen months, the assembly produced a new draft constitution, which enshrined social economic, and environmental

rights, overhauled the political system and introduced federalism. It did not, however, propose a republic, with the leaders of the Alliance of the Many eager to avoid turning the winnable referendum on the new constitution into a potentially challenging one on abolition of the monarchy. The new constitution was approved by over 60 per cent on the highest turnout in UK electoral history. The Alliance of the Many formed a political party, ready to contest the first elections under the new dispensation. There is much struggle ahead on a rapidly overheating planet, but perhaps we are leaving the time of monsters.

The purpose of these four futures is not to assert that we *will* win, but that we *can* win. Defeatism must be abandoned. We need both pessimism of the intellect and optimism of the will to develop our best strategy. Flexibility and openness must be our watchwords. I believe our side, the progressive side, will be much stronger if we are willing to work together and federate our forces into a proud left bloc.

Through federating our forces, we will be more effective agents for justice in society and we will be able to construct the party we need to enter the state. Once we come together, an advance in one area will add to the confidence of all. After all, confidence is what we need – bucketloads of it. If the many are to transform the world in their interests, they need to believe it's possible. It is the task of those on the left and in our movements to show not just that the current system is anti-human and heading towards frightening collapse, nor only that a more humane world is imaginable – but that we can actually get there.

If we do that, we have a planet to save and a world to win.

Notes

Introduction

1 The stay-and-fight position runs through the remaining Labour left, including its new/old standard-bearer, *Tribune* magazine. 'Many years of focus on street movements and minoritarian radicalism failed to grow our ranks or proliferate our ideas. Socialists should remember this, and stay in the Labour Party despite today's disappointment', argued editor Ronan Burtenshaw on the day of Keir Starmer's election as Labour leader ('Socialists: Stay in the Labour Party', *Tribune*, 4 April 2020). The founding statement of a new left network, Don't Leave, Organise, also urged 'all socialists to stay in the Party'. At the time of writing, its social media accounts have fallen silent.

2 'The Corbyn moment of 2017 is very unlikely to be repeated inside the Labour Party itself. It's a broken mirror . . . An Independent Labour Party with even half a dozen MPs and a membership base of perhaps 50,000 . . . could mark a real advance.' Tariq Ali, 'Starmer's War', *NLR/Sidecar*, 15 December 2020. 'The cost of inhabiting a house with diametrically opposed visions is paralysis . . . The left in Labour

needs to try something new, something different; something intellectually and politically post-Labour'. Mike Wayne, 'Roadmaps After Corbyn', *New Left Review* 131, September/October 2021, p. 65.

3 'The parliamentary road is closed and the institutional alliances it necessitated should be forsaken ... It was fruitless then and even more so now. The left's brief march through the institutions is over'. Jonas Marvin, 'The Left Won't Win the 2020s by Clinging to the Corpse of the Labour Party', Novara, 24 May 2021, a thoughtful response to an essay series I published on the same site. Joshua Virasami's *How To Change It* offers a useful guide to movement organising, with a strong focus on strategy, but electoral politics are absent from his plan for change. 'In Britain, so much self-described political activism happens away from the day-to-day conversations in communities ... If we want real power, people power, we need to be *with* our communities and workplaces in the struggle.' Joshua Virasami, *How to Change It: Making a Difference*, London, 2020, pp. 8–9. See also Charlie Kimber, 'It's Time to Leave Labour', *Socialist Worker*, 1 November 2020. 'Sealed tomb' is a phrase of Peter Mandleson's. See Lewis Minkin, *The Blair Supremacy: A Study in the Politics of Labour's Party Management*, Manchester, 2014, p. 378.

4 Enzo Traverso, *Left-Wing Melancholia: Marxism, History and Memory*, New York, 2017.

5 Labour last polled at 40 per cent in a Hanbury Strategy poll in April 2019.

6 Leo Panitch, 'A Decade on the Left', *Jacobin*, 3 July 2020; see also, with Sam Gindin, 'Class, Party and the Challenge of State Transformation', *Socialist Register*, vol. 53, 2017.

7 An April 2022 study by University College London's Constitution Unit found people feel 'frustrated' and 'let down'

by the British political system. See also Kate Proctor, 'Just 6% of UK Public "Want Return to Pre-pandemic Economy" ', *Guardian*, 29 June 2020.

8 Matt McGrath, 'Climate Change: IPCC Scientists Say It's "Now or Never" to Limit Warming', bbc.co.uk, 5 April 2022.

9 The article in question, 'How Life Could Change in 2030', authored by Danish politician Ida Auken and published on the World Economic Forum website, presented a cheery picture of a future world with no ownership or privacy, and a city with 'those we lost on the way' remaining outside its walls. After some uproar, the post was taken down, but is still available via the Wayback Machine.

10 Chuck Collins and Omar Ocampo, 'Global Billionaire Wealth Surges $4 Trillion over Pandemic', Institute for Policy Studies, 31 March 2021.

11 A study on the world's current capacity to substitute fossil fuels for renewables while retaining the energy consumption associated with our current level of societal demand for resources makes for sobering reading. See Simon P. Michaux, 'Assessment of the Extra Capacity Required of Alternative Energy Electrical Power Systems to Completely Replace Fossil Fuels', Geological Survey of Finland, August 2021.

12 'All we have to work with is the dreary bourgeois state, tethered to the circuits of capital as always. There would have to be popular pressure brought to bear on it, shifting the balance of forces condensed in it, forcing apparatuses to cut the tethers and begin to move.' Andreas Malm, *Corona, Climate, Chronic Emergency: War Communism in the Twenty-First Century*, London and New York, 2020, pp. 151–2.

13 Daniel Bensaïd, 'Leaps, Leaps, Leaps: Lenin and Politics', *International Socialism*, 95, July 2002.

14　See the chapter on 'The Modern Prince' in Antonio Gramsci, *Selections from the Prison Notebooks*, ed. and transl. Quintin Hoare and Geoffrey Nowell-Smith, London, 1971, especially p. 168.

15　In Gramsci's terminology, these phases are the 'war of manoeuvre' and the 'war of position'. Gramsci, *Selections from the Prison Notebooks*, for instance pp. 229–39.

1. The First Surge

1　Including me: I walked in off the street to volunteer in June 2015, hoping to do my small bit for a doomed but worthy campaign in a couple of weeks' break from my job as an Africa-focused journalist. By the end of the summer, Corbyn was leader, I had quit my job and along with Jon Lansman, Emma Rees and Adam Klug founded Momentum. After the 2016 leadership campaign, I joined Corbyn's leadership office working as spokesperson and head of strategic communications for the Labour Party until January 2020.

2　John McDonnell, 'What Now for the Left?', *Labour Briefing*, 27 May 2015.

3　Most notably in Alex Nunns, *The Candidate: Jeremy Corbyn's Improbable Path to Power*, London, 2016. Although Labour had degenerated a long way into the sort of cartel party anatomised by Peter Mair in *Ruling the Void: The Hollowing of Western Democracy* (London and New York, 2013), its surviving membership and democratic processes facilitated its revival as a mass organisation.

4　See Edmund Griffiths's blog post, 'The Great Leap Over the Institutions', 13 December 2019, for an interesting analysis of Corbynism based on such leaps. Griffiths argues that

'Corbynism may be defined as the attempt to replicate, at the level of state power, Corbyn's unexpected victory in the 2015 Labour leadership election'.

5 Max Shanly, 'New Model Young Labour', *Medium*, 20 November 2017 (originally a submission to the party's Democracy Review).

6 'UK Parliament Declares Climate Emergency', bbc.co.uk, 1 May 2019. On Labour for a Green New Deal, see Chris Saltmarsh, 'Green Socialism', in Grace Blakeley, ed., *Futures of Socialism*, London and New York, 2020, pp. 166–7.

7 Laclau elaborates on the role of the empty signifier in populist discourse construction. See Ernesto Laclau, *On Populist Reason*, London and New York, 2005, p. 28. I refer to Brexit as *semi*-floating, because the 'Take Back Control' slogan had an at least partially material basis.

8 'There is no such thing as Corbynism. There is socialism, there is social justice.' Jeremy Corbyn, speaking to the media on 13 December 2019.

2. Capital's A and B Teams

1 Tweeted by Adam Bienkov, chief Westminster correspondent for *Byline Times*, 30 September 2018 (@AdamBienkov).

2 As the *Guardian*'s political editor wrote in her despatch from the Tory conference, 'Sometimes it felt as though Jeremy Corbyn's name was as much on people's lips here, as in Liverpool – and not just as a cartoonish throwback to the winter of discontent, but as a genuine political threat. Labour's analysis of what's wrong in Britain – stagnant real wages, towns left behind by globalisation, a political system out of touch with the public – in many ways framed the discussions in Birmingham.' Heather Stewart, 'Opportunity

Knocks: What We Learned from the Tory Conference', *Guardian*, 3 October 2018.

3 In this novel about the impact of the Risorgimento on aristocratic life in Sicily, Tancredi, beloved nephew of the Prince of Salina, joins Garibaldi's Redshirts. Explaining his actions, Tancredi tells his uncle that 'for everything to stay the same, everything must change'.

4 Karl Marx, 'The Eighteenth Brumaire of Louis Napoleon', in *The Political Writings*, London and New York, 2019, p. 565.

5 A Survation poll published on 11 April put the Conservatives on 37 per cent and Labour on 41 per cent. By the end of the month, YouGov had both parties on 29 per cent. By the middle of June, YouGov had them both on just 20 per cent, narrowly behind both the Liberal Democrats and the Brexit Party.

6 See Antonio Gramsci, *Selections from the Prison Notebooks*, ed. and transl. Quintin Hoare and Geoffrey Nowell Smith, London, 1971, pp. 219ff.

7 According to Nixon's madman theory, a leader may encourage advisors and intermediaries to present him or her as mad and liable to take extreme measures, whether in warfare or negotiations. In Nixon's case, this posture allowed the Vietnamese and Soviets to believe he was willing to use nuclear weapons.

8 Thomas Colson, 'Remainer MPs Are Plotting to Bring Down Boris Johnson's Government, Install a "Unity" Prime Minister, and Delay Brexit', *Business Insider*, 6 August 2019; 'What Is a National Unity Government and Who Would Lead It?', *The Week*, 7 October 2019; Polly Toynbee, 'Only a Government of National Unity Can Deliver Us from No Deal', *Guardian*, 5 August 2019.

9 Labour Party draft papers on framing Tory leadership candidates, May and June 2019.

10 See Tom Gann, 'Fuck Business: Johnsonism, Hegemony and the Popular Classes', *New Socialist*, 25 August 2020, for an interesting discussion of Johnsonism that also draws on 'The Eighteenth Brumaire' and a Gramscian analysis of class fractions.

11 Stefan Boscia, 'Boris Johnson Calls on the Private Sector to Rebuild Britain after Covid', *City AM*, 6 October 2020.

12 Johnson performed a similar routine as mayor of London, bringing back the Routemaster bus and unleashing a wave of construction projects by relaxing planning regulations – and, of course, making fortunes for developers in the process.

13 David Roediger, *The Wages of Whiteness: Race and the Making of the American Working Class*, revd edn, London and New York, 2007.

14 Adam Almeida, 'The Government Must Not Use Pseudo-Science to Dismiss Covid's Impact on BME Communities', Runnymede Trust, 25 January 2021.

15 'Who Do You Hold Responsible for the Rise in Coronavirus Cases over the Last Month?', YouGov, 11 January 2021.

16 Leah Sinclair, 'Police Guard Statue of Winston Churchill as Protesters Gather around Monument Chanting "Protect Women, Not Statues"', *Evening Standard*, 15 March 2021.

17 Regarding the juggling trick, see the closing description of Louis Napoleon in Marx's 'The Eighteenth Brumaire', in *The Political Writings*, p. 565: 'Driven by the contradictory demands of his situation, and being at the same time, like a juggler, under the necessity of keeping the public gaze on himself . . . by springing constant surprises – that is to say, under the necessity of arranging a coup d'état in miniature every day – Bonaparte throws the whole bourgeois economy

into confusion . . . and produces anarchy in the name of order, while at the same time stripping the entire state machinery of its halo, profaning it and making it at once loathsome and ridiculous.' As for double-dealing with the status quo, we can see this approach in Johnson's handling of social care. Deflecting calls for a wealth tax that would have stung the Tory base, in September 2021 he announced a fix for this perennially stuck policy issue by requiring younger workers to 'save the NHS' and effectively cover the care costs of older homeowners through higher National Insurance contributions.

18 Johnson has previously taken the distinctly non-populist line that 'nobody has stuck up for the bankers as much as me'. Nick Duffy, 'Boris Johnson Says Nobody "Stuck Up for the Bankers as Much as I Did" when Asked about "F**k Business" Jibe', *i News*, 22 June 2019.

19 Cummings uses his blog to excoriate his former boss for deviating from the 'people's government'-course that Cummings' Vote Leave team set for Johnson. Cummings wants Johnson replaced as prime minister, and by the close of 2021 put the odds of that happening in 2022 at 80 per cent.

20 The story first broke on 1 December 2021 in the *Mirror*.

21 He lost his chief of staff Dan Rosenfeld, principal private secretary Martin Reynolds, communications director Jack Doyle and press secretary Allegra Stratton. Before partygate, 29 per cent of the public thought Johnson was doing a good job as prime minister, falling to 22 per cent at the scandal's January peak, according to YouGov. The North Shropshire by-election, held on 16 December 2021 to replace Owen Paterson, was won by Liberal Democrat Helen Morgan, who came from third, leapfrogging Labour, to win on a huge 34.2 per cent swing. On 19 January, Bury South MP Christian

Wakeford crossed the floor and joined Labour citing his lack of confidence in the prime minister. If fifty-four Conservative MPs write letters to the party's 1922 Committee, it would trigger a no-confidence vote. In January and February of 2022, speculation was rife over how many had sent in letters, with most media estimates ranging from twenty to thirty.

22 'Today's fine might not mean Boris Johnson goes immediately, because the political temperature around this is lower than in February', wrote Sky's deputy political editor Sam Coates (@SamCoatesSky) on Twitter.

23 Rory Scothorne, 'Under New Management', *London Review of Books*, 13 August 2020.

24 Tellingly, the largest numerical rebellion against Corbyn's leadership was over a 2016 vote he forced in Parliament to ban arms sales to Saudi Arabia due to its brutal war in Yemen. Almost a hundred Labour MPs failed to back the motion. With this balance of forces in the party, Corbyn's long-held support for peace-oriented policies such as ditching nuclear weapons and Britain's membership in NATO could not be achieved.

25 As a member of Starmer's shadow cabinet, Ed Miliband has advocated a Green New Deal, including the public ownership of energy, water and transport, saying it was 'the right way to go' in an interview on BBC's *Newsnight*. Despite the commitments Starmer himself made in his leadership election, his office was furious. At conference, Starmer used his marquee interview with Andrew Marr to reject public ownership outright. In a reshuffle in November 2021, Starmer stripped Miliband of the business half of his brief. And on 11 April 2022, Labour called on the government to ban protests at oil terminals and across Britain's road network and make it easier for the police to arrest climate protesters.

26 Comparing YouGov tracker polls. See also 'Are Voters Starting to Lose Patience with Starmer?', YouGov, 29 September 2021.

27 Anne McElvoy, 'Keir Starmer Is Making Headway, but Has He Got Enough to Worry the Tories?', *Guardian*, 2 January 2022. See also Dominic Cummings, 'How Could Labour Win? Swap Dud "Dead Player" Starmer for a Midlands Woman', *Substack*, 20 October 2021, in which he argues 'keeping Starmer is an all-in gamble on Boris self-destructing'.

28 The soft left, who cheerled Starmer in 2020 through its faction Open Labour and received top jobs in his first shadow cabinet, are the vanishing mediator between Corbynism and a full Blairite restoration, in a clear analogue to the 1980s and 1990s.

29 In early March 2022, Starmer forced eleven Labour MPs to withdraw their names from a Stop the War statement that pre-dated Russia's invasion of Ukraine (but which he presented as post-invasion) or lose the whip. Within an hour, all eleven did so and John McDonnell and Diane Abbott both pulled out of speaking at Stop the War events. Corbyn, with no whip left to lose, continues to support Stop the War.

30 Labour's headquarters from 1994 to 2002 was in Millbank Tower, Westminster.

31 The Socialist Campaign Group comprises thirty-five MPs and four members of the House of Lords.

32 The fractiousness of the Labour left was demonstrated by its failure to agree on effective slates for internal party elections through the Centre Left Grassroots Alliance or to run joint campaigns thereafter.

33 In the May 2021 by-election for a PLP position on the NEC, Angela Eagle, the candidate of the right, received 150 votes to Grahame Morris's 38.

34 This labourism has been described as 'an ideology of decent

and dignified subordination'. Hilary Wainwright, *A Tale of Two Parties*, London, 1986, p. 294.

35 Anoosh Chakelian, 'Peter Mandelson: I'm Afraid Keir Starmer Has Come Badly Unstuck', *New Statesman*, 11 May 2021.

3. Our Bloc

1 'Key Time Series: British Social Attitudes 37', NatCen Social Research, 2020.

2 Royal Mail up 7 points to 69 per cent, water supply up 6 points to 63 per cent, buses up 9 points to 55 per cent.

3 In the run-up to the 1983 general election, the SDP–Liberal Alliance won a series of striking by-elections and reached 50 per cent in opinion polls. But, come election day, Thatcher had restored her support through victory in the Falklands and the alliance won twenty-three seats to Labour's 209, despite receiving just 2 per cent fewer votes. A similar pattern, although less stark, repeated itself in 2010. Following the first leaders' debate, the Lib Dems outpolled Labour, and for a few days pulled ahead of the Conservatives too. But despite claiming 23 per cent of the vote, the Liberal Democrats ended up actually losing seats, winning just 57 out of 650.

4 See Leo Panitch and Colin Leys, *Searching for Socialism: The Project of the Labour New Left from Benn to Corbyn*, London and New York, 2020, pp. 96–8. Tariq Ali wrote in the early 1980s that Tony Benn 'understood that Labour's only serious electoral chance lies in turning the entire organization into a giant lever of popular political mobilizations, championing the causes of all sectors of the oppressed, and offering a governmental perspective of real change'. Ali, 'Why I'm Joining the Labour Party', *Socialist Review*, 38, 1981, pp. 20–1.

5   Katrina Forrester, 'By Leaps or by Federation: Two Paths to Left Unity', *South Atlantic Quarterly*, 120: 4, 2021.

6   Ralph Miliband, 'Counter-Hegemonic Struggles', *Socialist Register*, 26, 1990, reprinted *Jacobin*, 20 June 2018.

7   'There exists a vast discrepancy between the message which [ruling class] hegemonic endeavours seek to disseminate, and the actual reality which daily confronts the vast majority of the population for whom the message is mainly intended. The message speaks of democracy, equality, opportunity, prosperity, security, community, common interests, justice, fairness, etc. The reality, on the other hand, as lived by the majority, is very different, and includes the experience of exploitation, domination, great inequalities in all spheres of life, material constraints of all kinds, and very often great spiritual want. Reality may not be conceived and articulated in these precise terms, but it is nevertheless adversely felt, and produces frustration, alienation, anger, dissent, and pressure from below for the resolution of grievances.' Miliband, 'Counter-Hegemonic Struggles'.

8   'What's the Legacy of this Year's Black Lives Matter Protests?', YouGov, 23 December 2020; YouGov ratings, Q3 2021. These were demonstrations against the government's Police, Crime, Sentencing and Courts Bill, a new law which restricts the right to protest if those actions cause 'annoyance' and increases sentences for property damage.

9   'This from a Conservative official [Ben Goldsmith, chair of the Conservative Environment Network and a director at Defra] is an insult to people facing misery trying to get to work. While the government continues to refuse to act, Labour has called for immediate injunctions to put a stop to this disruption.' Tweeted by Sam Coates, deputy political editor of *Sky News* (@SamCoatesSky), 12 April 2022.

10 Office for National Statistics, 'Trade Union Membership, UK 1995–2020: Statistical Bulletin', 27 May 2021. Women are now more likely to be in a union than men and make up half the total number of union members. Britain's two biggest unions, Unison and Unite, both have female general secretaries for the first time.

11 'Work in 2021: A Tale of Two Economies', CLASS, May 2021. The GMB, another of the big general unions, led a forty-four-day strike in 2021 against British Gas, which also was seeking to use fire and rehire. Unison, on the other hand, has relied on the strength of its legal department more than industrial action to advance workers' interests, winning £124 million for NHS members in unpaid holiday pay and a Court of Appeal ruling that employers must consult unions on workplace changes that affect members.

12 In the 2010s Unite was involved in four times as many industrial action ballots than every other British trade union combined: Len McCluskey, *Always Red*, London, 2021, p. 289. In Graham's first hundred days in charge the union claims to have won forty-three pay deals worth £25 million for 12,000 workers, many gaining above-inflation wage increases. In three-quarters of cases, the dispute was won when Unite members either voted for strike action or because strikes had forced the employer to improve its offer. Randeep Ramesh, 'Unite Will Use "Brains as Well as Brawn" to Fight Bad Employers, Says Boss', *Guardian*, 2 December 2021. Two other left-led unions, the CWU and PCS, are well represented in critical sectors of the economy: communications and public administration.

13 Starmer endorsed this effort in 2019, but by 2021 was refusing to back a minimum wage of £15 per hour, despite 59 per cent of Tory voters saying they back the increase and only 23 per cent opposed. Jon Stone, 'Voters of All Parties

Overwhelmingly Support £15 Minimum Wage, Poll Finds', *Independent*, 30 September 2021.

14 In February 2021, the UK Supreme Court ruled that Uber drivers are employees, not self-employed, striking a major blow to the company's exploitative business model. For background, see Callum Cant, *Riding for Deliveroo: Resistance in the New Economy*, Cambridge, 2020.

15 There are US precedents: for example, the Los Angeles teachers strike of 2019 saw a merging of worker and community demands leading to a 6 per cent pay rise, an increase in support staff and reduced class sizes. Educators were on strike *for* their students, their parents and the wider community, not against them.

16 Author's calculations based on Office for National Statistics data. There is also significant regional variation in union membership density: 35 per cent of employees in Merseyside are in a union; for Inner London, the rate is just 18 per cent. Union members have become much older. In 1995, a third of union members were under thirty-five; now it's just a quarter. Only 23 per cent were over fifty; now it's 39 per cent.

17 This caused apoplexy in the Tory press. Ben Riley-Smith, 'How the Unions Wrote Corbyn's Manifesto: More Than 100 Demands "Copied and Pasted" into Labour's Draft', *Telegraph*, 13 May 2017.

18 NEU membership increased by 36,000, and an astonishing half a million people attended one union zoom call. 'Work in 2021: A Tale of Two Economies', CLASS, May 2021.

19 Richard Partington, 'Unemployment Figures Should Be 3m Higher, Says Research', *Guardian*, 17 October 2019.

20 'Rebuilding Communities by the Many', internal COU review of 2019 general election results.

21 The campaign itself is co-convened by two federations, the Progressive International, a global network of progressive movements, unions, parties and people, and UNI Global Union, a federation representing 20 million workers across 150 countries.

22 Patrick Collinson, 'UK Tenants Paid Record £50 Billion in Rents in 2017', *Guardian*, 12 February 2018.

23 The social model of disability holds that society disables people with impairments. For more on this subject see Ellen Clifford, *The War on Disabled People: Capitalism, Welfare and the Making of a Human Catastrophe*, London, 2020.

24 Donald Read, *The English Provinces, c. 1760–1960: A Study in Influence*, London, 1964, p. 214.

25 Rodrigo Nunes, *Neither Vertical nor Horizontal: A Theory of Political Organisation*, London and New York, 2021, pp. 13, 65–6.

4. Movement Populism

1 'By directing popular anger toward the top and encouraging working people's resistance from below, Sanders's democratic socialist message inspired people across lines of difference to unite in solidarity against their common enemy.' Meagan Day and Micah Uetricht, *Bigger Than Bernie: How We Can Win Democratic Socialism in Our Time*, London and New York, 2021, p. 213.

2 Chantal Mouffe, *For a Left Populism*, London and New York, 2018, p. 24. The creation of an *us* requires, in Mouffe's and Laclau's terminology, 'a chain of equivalence among the demands of the workers, the immigrants and the precarious middle class, as well as other democratic demands, such as those of the LGBT community'.

3 See Donald Trump's 'Arguments for America', the closing video of the 2016 campaign, for extremely effective and transversal right-populist communications. It ends, 'The only thing that can stop this corrupt machine is you. The only force strong enough to save our country is us. The only people brave enough to vote out this corrupt establishment is you, the American people. I'm doing this for the people and for the movement and we will take back this country for you and we will make America great again.' Or Marine Le Pen's 2017 campaign video, which employs similar transversal right-populist appeals but in the particular vernacular of French politics.

4 Ernesto Laclau and Chantal Mouffe, *Hegemony and Socialist Strategy: Towards a Radical Democratic Politics*, 2nd edn, London and New York, 2014, p. 160.

5 Various substantive formulations have been tried in different political contexts. Podemos used *la casta*, meaning the establishment. 'The people' is a hardy perennial, but I hold that 'the many versus the few' is the strongest frame we have available – the many is, by definition, not homogeneous.

6 Mouffe, *For a Left Populism*, p. 80.

7 Chantal Mouffe, 'Why a Populist Left Should Rally around a Green Democratic Transformation', Open Democracy, 15 September 2020. See also Mouffe's *Towards a Green Democratic Revolution*, forthcoming.

8 The announcement in Corbyn's conference speech of 2018 of a 'green jobs revolution' of 400,000 jobs in green industries such as insulation has been the most eye-catching to date.

9 The 2019 manifesto opened with the section on 'Green Industrial Revolution', with chapters on energy, transport, environment, animal welfare and regional strategies. These

policies had more detailed papers sitting behind them, such as 'Bringing Energy Home' and 'Thirty Recommendations for 2030'.

10 'When do we start physically attacking the things that consume our planet and destroy them with our own hands? Is there a good reason we have waited this long?' Andreas Malm, *How to Blow Up a Pipeline: Learning to Fight in a World on Fire*, London and New York, 2021, p. 9.

11 Insulate Britain's actions were opposed by 72 per cent of people: 'Three Weeks into Motorway Climate Change Protests, Public Opposition Has Only Grown', YouGov, 8 October 2021. I would argue that minoritarian and counterproductive action would be less likely to occur after the formation of the left bloc. First, the very process of coming together breeds majoritarianism and the recognition of different issues. But second, if the action were raised at a meeting with other groups, it would have been advised against.

12 Conversely, without Fridays for Future giving a friendly face to the climate movement, XR would be written off as fringe or extreme – 'crusties', in Boris Johnson's lexicon.

13 The 'beyond politics' comment comes from the last tweet written by David Graeber, an ally of XR, who took this tendency to task before his untimely death in 2020.

14 In Gramscian terms, this is a shift in the mechanisms of rule from consent to domination. See Ranajit Guha, *Dominance without Hegemony*, Cambridge, MA, 1997; and Perry Anderson, *The H Word: The Peripeteia of Hegemony*, London and New York, 2017, which discusses Guha's contribution to the theory of hegemony.

15 This offers an example of how a slogan may achieve its meaning through a political process. On the contrary, Labour's 2017 election slogan, 'For the Many, Not the Few', took a

Blair-era slogan that was designed to empty Labour of its class content and instead reinscribed it with populist antagonism.

16 We should be aware that the trick of the right is to turn an issue into a row about process, rather than the underlying subject. Hence there is more media analysis of protestors' tactics than of what they are protesting about.

17 My calculation based on comparing the *Sunday Times* Rich List at the start and end of the decade, and real average wages with projected wages (if they had increased in line with trend growth rather than stagnated).

18 This removal of 'unfettered sovereignty in the economic sphere' was an explicit aim of the neoliberal thinkers. F. A. Hayek, *The Road to Serfdom*, London, 2014, p. 238. For a history of neoliberal thinkers see Quinn Slobodian, *Globalists: The End of Empire and the Birth of Neoliberalism*, Cambridge, MA, April 2018.

19 For example, the Bank of England could use quantitative easing to lend new money at extremely low rates to a Green Policy Bank, which would be mandated to invest to secure decarbonisation and jobs throughout the country.

20 For a critical history of the BBC and government influence over it, see Tom Mills, *The BBC: Myth of a Public Service*, London and New York, 2016.

21 Dominic Penna, 'BBC May Not Exist in a Decade, Says Nadine Dorries as She Hits Out at "Left-Wing Bias" ', *Telegraph*, 4 October 2021.

22 Personal correspondence with Matt Turner, then *Evolve* political editor, 22 November 2021. See also Robert Booth, 'DIY Political Websites: New Force Shaping the General Election Debate', *Guardian*, 1 June 2017.

23 Emma Roth, 'Twitter's Research Shows that its Algorithm Favors Conservative Views', *Verge*, 22 October 2021.

24 Craig Silverman, Ryan Mac and Pranav Dixit, 'A Whistle-blower Says Facebook Ignored Global Political Manipulation', *Buzzfeed*, 14 September 2020.

25 The reality at the time was that just 0.6 per cent of girls under sixteen got pregnant, 0.7 per cent of the benefit bill was lost to fraud, the pensions bill was nearly ten times that of development aid, 5 per cent of the population were Muslim and 13–15 per cent of the population were migrants. 'Perceptions Are Not Reality', Ipsos MORI, 9 July 2013.

26 Survation, fieldwork 15 March 2019. See also Greg Philo, Mike Berry, Justin Schlosberg, Anthony Lerman and David Miller, *Bad News for Labour: Antisemitism, the Party and Public Belief*, London, 2019.

27 'Post-Covid Policy', YouGov/NEON, fieldwork 7–11 May 2020.

28 Lawrence White, 'British Public Don't Trust Banks 10 Years After Crisis, Survey Finds', Reuters, 16 August 2018; 'Public Attitudes Towards Amazon', Survation, 25 November 2020.

29 'New Poll Shows Huge Public Support for Decisive Action to Make the Gig Economy Fairer', Fairwork, 28 October 2021.

30 'Jeremy Corbyn Is on the Right Side of Public Opinion on Foreign Policy: Except for the Falklands', YouGov, 30 May 2017.

31 Polling shows Corbyn's leadership advanced public attitudes on public ownership and other issues in a progressive direction. Jon Stone, 'Public Support for Nationalisation Increased while Jeremy Corbyn Was Labour Leader, Poll Finds', *Independent*, 16 December 2019.

32 'Trust in Media 2021', European Broadcasting Union, 2 September 2021.

33 There were 8 million unique views of a Momentum video on Facebook in 2021. It is an indictment of the corporate

media and a powerful argument for its independent cousin that stories of corruption and dodgy PPE contracts have come from the dogged work of independents, such as *Byline Times.*

34 'The left could do worse than begin by "learning from Thatcherism". Now, nothing is more calculated to drive the left into a tizzy than this scandalous proposition. It is a sign both of the defensiveness and the residual sectarianism of the left that it misreads an injunction to analyse "Thatcherism" for a recommendation to swallow it whole. It is time to correct this fatal confusion, most of all because it is now so politically disabling. Unless the left can understand Thatcherism . . . it cannot renew itself because it cannot understand the world it must live in.' Stuart Hall, *The Hard Road to Renewal: Thatcherism and the Crisis of the Left,* London and New York, 2021 [1988], p. 272.

35 For an example of this working for the left, see the high levels of coverage of Labour's 2017 manifesto because it was leaked and contained clear winners (the many) and losers (the few). Regarding the right, in the 2016 US presidential election Trump received additional coverage estimated at $5 billion in value by data tracking firm MediaQuant.

36 This involved two thousand bookings in 2021, according to the group's executive director Dan Vockins.

37 This has been termed the 'strategic field'. Nicos Poulantzas, *State, Power, Socialism,* London and New York, 2014.

38 Greg Philo and Mike Berry, '*Bad News for Labour:* A response to Channel 4's "FactCheck"', Jewish Voice for Labour, 3 November 2020.

39 Bernard Lewis, *Semites and Anti-semites,* London, 1986; Jonathan Sacks, 'Rabbi Sacks on the Connection between Antisemitism, Anti-Zionism, Judaism and Israel', YouTube,

2019. Prominent scholars who reject this notion include Anthony Lerman and Brian Klug.

40 Interviewed in *Forced Out*, 2019, available on YouTube.

41 Owen Hatherley, *Red Metropolis: Socialism and the Government of London*, London, 2020.

42 A full 80 per cent of global trade takes place in these value chains linked to multinational companies. 'GVCs and Development: Investment and Value Added Trade in the Global Economy', UNCTAD, 2013.

43 'Comparing Debt Payments with Health Spending', Jubilee Debt Campaign, April 2020.

44 Alexander Kentikelenis and Thomas Stubbs, 'Austerity Redux: The Post-pandemic Wave of Budget Cuts and the Future of Global Public Health', *Global Policy*, 23 November 2021.

45 'Mega-rich recoup Covid-losses in record-time yet billions will live in poverty for at least a decade', Oxfam, 25 January 2021.

46 'Trade and Development Report 2020', UNCTAD, 2020.

47 Zoltán Kis and Zain Rizvi, 'How to Make Enough Vaccine for the World in One Year', *Public Citizen*, 26 May 2021.

5. Party and State

1 Chantal Mouffe, *For a Left Populism*, London and New York, 2018, p. 20. For a lively discussion on Podemos, populism and post-financial crisis politics, see Inigo Errejon and Chantal Mouffe, *Podemos: In the Name of the People*, London, 2016. Errejon was Podemos's political secretary when this book was written.

2 Jeremy Gilbert made a similar argument in an article emailed

to Momentum members. Jeremy Gilbert, 'Why We Shouldn't Leave the Labour Party', 15 December 2021.

3 Max Shanly, a socialist active in the Corbyn movement, is an exception. He has thought substantially, although published little, on these questions, and his proposals are worth reading. See Max Shanly, 'Towards a New Model Young Labour', Medium, 20 November 2017. Tom Blackburn, another socialist active in the Corbyn movement, developed ideas for party transformation under the rubric of 'Corbynism from below'. It was to be brought together in a book, until rendered obsolete by the 2019 election defeat. The valuable thinking contained within it would usefully be repurposed for this 'new model' party blueprint work.

4 The motion called for private schools to be integrated into the state sector, as well as policies short of integration: taxing private schools more heavily and reducing their students' access to university.

5 For analysis of the state's class character and space for contestation, see: Ralph Miliband, *The State in Capitalist Society*, London, 2009 (1969); Göran Therborn, *What Does the Ruling Class Do When It Rules?*, London and New York, 2007; and Poulantzas, *State, Power, Socialism*. For an assessment of the famous debate between Miliband and Poulantzas, see Bob Jessop, 'Dialogue of the Deaf: Reflections on the Poulantzas-Miliband Debate', in P. Wetherly, C. W. Barrow and P. Burnham, eds, *Class, Power and the State in Capitalist Society: Essays on Ralph Miliband*, Basingstoke, 2007.

6 See for example, Peter Mayo, 'In and against the State: Gramsci, a War of Position and Adult Education', in *Hegemony and Education under Neoliberalism: Insights from Gramsci*, London, 2015.

7 Leo Panitch and Sam Gindin, 'In and against the State', *Red*

Pepper, 'Creating the Future', special issue with The World Transformed, 1 October 2018.

8 André Gorz, 'Reform and Revolution', *Socialist Register* 5, 1968.

9 'Medicines for the Many: Public Health Before Private Profit', UK Labour Party, September 2019.

10 We are being warned that the politics accompanying these dramatic environmental changes could be equally dystopian. See Andreas Malm and the Zetkin Collective, *White Skin, Black Fuel: On the Danger of Fossil Fascism*, London and New York, 2021.

6. Ways of Winning

1 'The actual trajectory of large-scale social change that we observe in history is the result of the interaction of two kinds of change-generating processes: first, the cumulative unintended by-products of the actions of people operating under existing social relations, and second, the cumulative intended effects of conscious projects of social change by people acting strategically to transform those social relations.' Erik Olin Wright, *Envisioning Real Utopias*, London and New York, 2010, p. 298.

2 Olin Wright, *Envisioning Real Utopias*, pp. 303ff.

3 With apologies to the social-science fiction of Peter Frase, *Four Futures: Visions of the World After Capitalism*, London and New York, 2016.